GW00994200

JEP

Rothman Foundation Series

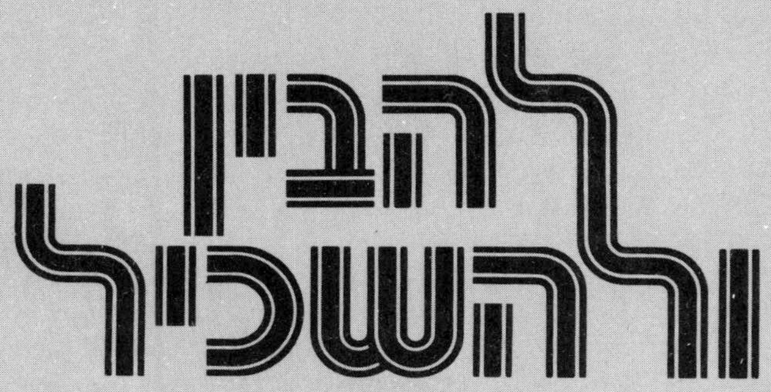

A GUIDE TO TORAH HASHKOFOH

QUESTIONS AND ANSWERS ON JUDAISM

Rabbi Eliezer Gevirtz

JEWISH EDUCATION PROGRAM
425 East 9th Street
Brooklyn, New York 11218
212-941-2600

First Printing May 1980
Second Printing November 1980

First Israel Printing 1988

Sole Trade Distributors
PHILIPP FELDHEIM, INC.
200 Airport Executive Park
Spring Valley, NY 10977

FELDHEIM PUBLISHERS Ltd.
POB 6525
Jerusalem, Israel

ISBN 0-87306-975-7

Printed in Israel

In memory of

Henry I. Rothman ז״ל

and

Bertha G. Rothman ע״ה

לחמו מלחמות ה׳

"who lived and fought
for Torah-true Judaism"

Published through the courtesy of the
HENRY, BERTHA and EDWARD ROTHMAN FOUNDATION
Rochester, N.Y. • Circleville, Ohio • Cleveland

Other volumes in the
Jewish Education Program—Rothman Foundation Series

Lilmod Ul'lamed

from the teachings of our Sages . . .
a compendium of insights, homilies, and interpretations of the weekly Sedra.

by: Rabbi Mordechai Katz

L'hovin Ul'haskil

a guide to Torah Hashkofoh . . .
Questions and answers on Judaism.

by: Rabbi Eliezer Gevirtz

Lishmor V'Laasos

a guide to basic principles of Jewish law and their applications in theory and in practice . . .

by: Rabbi Mordechai Katz

Menucha V'Simcha

a guide to basic laws and themes of Shabbos and Yom Tov . . .

by: Rabbi Mordechai Katz

. . . available in softcover, clothbound,
or handsomely designed, four-volume, gift set.

Jewish Education Program

The Joseph & Faye Tanenbaum Jewish Education Program of Zeirei Agudath Israel was organized in September 1972, and since its inception has become a well-known, active force in the field of Jewish education. Its guiding principle, "Jewish power and Jewish pride through Jewish education," was formulated in response to what has become a Jewish tragedy of massive proportions, namely assimilation and its tragic by-products.

Under the guidelines of prominent Roshei Yeshivos and leaders in the field of Jewish education, and staffed entirely by B'nei Torah and Yeshiva graduates, JEP relies almost entirely on the talents and efforts voluntarily contributed by capable young Torah students.

Some of JEP's programs include: Shabbatones, in which hundreds of children from various communities in the United States and Canada experience the beauty of Shabbos in a Torah true environment; Release Hour classes for spiritually-starved public school children; programs for needy Russian immigrants; Ruach and Seminar sessions for day school students; Chavruso Big Brother Programs; High School Encounter Groups; Holiday Rallies; Yeshiva and Camp Placement; and the publication of educational material for thousands of young people. Through these and other various programs, JEP hopes to ignite the spark of Yiddishkeit deep within the hearts of these individuals, and turn it into a blazing, warmth-emanating fire. It hopes to instill within these youngsters a love of Hashem and His Torah and an understanding of Torah-true Judaism.

משה פיינשטיין
ר"מ תפארת ירושלים
בנוא יארק

RABBI MOSES FEINSTEIN
455 F. D. R. DRIVE
NEW YORK, N. Y. 10002
OREGON 7-1222

בע"ה

הנה מכבר הובא לפני ספר ללמוד וללמד שהו"ל איחוד ה"תכנית לחינוך היהודי" הנודע בשם "דשעפ" בשביל מטרתם לחזק לבות הרחוקים ולגלות לעיניהם מתק אור תורתינו הקדושה מתוך חומר חינוכי גדוש מאמרי חז"ל מצות ודינים וכדו', ואמרתי אז יישר חילם לאורייתא.

ועתה הוסיפו להו"ל ספר חדש כשמו כן הוא "להבין ולהשכיל" לבות הצעירים ביסודות הדת והשקפות תורתינו ולהראותם עושר יקר תפארת אמונתנו הקדושה להמשיכם בעבותות האהבה והיראה לתוך מחנינו, מחנה התורה בע"ה. והנני בזה לאשר ולחזק ידיהם של כל העוסקים בעבודת החבורה הדגולה ההיא ויהי"ר שתשרה שכינה במעשה ידיהם.

משה פיינשטיין

ACKNOWLEDGMENTS

An undertaking such as this cannot be the work of one individual alone.

It is therefore with deep gratitude that I graciously thank all those who have assisted in its preparation.

The **Jewish Education Program** is a project whose aims deserve the support of all concerned Jews. Its directors have worked tirelessly to ignite the spark of *Yiddishkeit* in those unaware of it. They deserve credit as the prime movers behind this publication.

Rabbi Mordechai Katz, the eminently talented founder of JEP, provided the original impetus for a *hashkofoh* work of this sort, and arranged the basic draft of its format.

Rabbi Yosef Chaim Golding, JEP's present vigorous executive director, spent untold time and effort seeing to it that this work would be properly produced and made available to the public.

Their interest and inspiration are what made this publication possible. May they continue to devote their supreme abilities to the furtherance of *Yiddishkeit* among Jewish youth. The Jewish world greatly needs their help.

We are greatly indebted to the Henry, Bertha, and Edward Rothman Foundation for sponsoring this publication in memory of their parents. May *Hashem* grant them continued success in all of their worthy endeavors and may they continue to spread Jewish education to those who so desperately need it.

At the same time, I would like to thank the leaders of Agudath Israel of America, JEP's parent body, without whose backing JEP could not exist.

A work such as this must be guided by *Da'as Torah.* To insure this, JEP's directors asked several eminent Roshei Yeshiva to assist, and they responded with a graciousness and cooperation that was all the more remarkable in view of their extremely busy schedules. I would therefore like to thank Horav Yisroel Belsky, *shlita,* Rosh Yeshiva from Yeshiva Torah Vodaath; Horav Joseph Elias, *shlita,* Principal, Rika Breuer's Seminary; and Horav Reuven Feinstein, *shlita,* Rosh Hayeshiva, Mesivta Tifereth Yerusholaim, Staten Island, New York, for taking the time to read the material and offer their sagacious comments and suggestions, which have been incorporated into the text.

I would also like to thank Rabbi Nisson Wolpin, editor of the

Jewish Observer, Mr. Danny Gross, Miss Sandy Silbermintz, and Mr. Yitzchok Feldheim, of Feldheim Publishers, for their proofreading and invaluable advice throughout the writing of this book.

The *seforim* of Horav Avigdor Miller, *shlita*, were also especially useful in the preparation of this work, and many of the examples contained herein were inspired by his ideas. The reader is strongly advised to consult Rav Miller's *seforim* for additional insights into Jewish hashkofoh.

Deep appreciation also goes to Nutti Goldbrenner and Shiya Markowitz of M. & G. Art Design for their invaluable technical assistance in putting together this book and for making JEP's educational series a reality.

I would also like to thank Tovia Ganz and Yaakov Lock of Light Medium & Bold Typesetting for a wonderful job.

We must also acknowledge and thank Mr. Max Septimus for allowing us to, utilize his priceless library collection for the front covers of JEP's educational series.

Special thanks to Mrs. Malky Bodenstein and Mrs. Chavy Aranoff who typed the original manuscript and to Mr. Shmuel Shpelfogel for his technical assistance.

I would like to thank my Rebbeim and teachers for their guidance and encouragement throughout the years; and to my students at Yeshiva Ahiezer and Yeshiva Rabbi Samson Raphael Hirsch for helping me define many of the ideas in this book.

Finally, I would like to pay public tribute to my parents, Mr. and Mrs. Sidney Gevirtz, and the rest of my family who have helped me, advised me and guided me throughout my life.

May *Hashem* grant them the spiritual well-being that they so richly deserve.

Rabbi Eliezer Gevirtz

New York, N.Y.
Nissan, 5740

PREFACE

ותן בליבנו **להבין ולהשכיל** לשמוע ללמוד
וללמד לשמור ולעשות ולקיים את כל דברי
תלמוד תורתך באהבה: (תפילת שחרית)

"And put it into our hearts ***to gain insight and understanding,*** *to hear, to learn and to teach, to observe, to do and to fulfill with love all the words of the tradition of Your Torah." (Morning Prayers)*

Understanding. A rare commodity today.

It is true that our age has more information than any other before it. Mass media and computers have seen to it that the average man today has plentiful data at his fingertips. Scientists have made sure that we know more facts about the world than we ever thought possible.

And yet . . .

For all the facts, for all the data, full comprehension of life seems further away than ever. Our present world condition proves it. We know secrets of the atom that our ancestors never dreamed of; yet, we have mainly used this information to make weapons of war. We have abundant data on the human body and the human psyche—we can cure physical ills and diagnose mental conditions—yet man is at least as destructive and depressed as ever. Rivalries, tensions, unhappiness all abound. The life of peace and harmony that we should have established by now seems more remote with each passing generation.

Part of the problem may be that man seems unable to make sense of all that lies before him. He appears stymied by the central question: What is life for, and how should it be lived? Without an answer to this, without an approach to proper living, existence can indeed seem puzzling.

Judaism has its own philosophy of life, based on G-d's Torah. Jews throughout the centuries have used it as their guide to basic life questions. It has enhanced their lives with meaning even during the darkest of days.

But today, with life so complex and so problematic, even many Jews may be confused. Can the Torah still provide relevant answers to the questions of the twenty-first century?

We feel that it can.

This book has been prepared by the Jewish Education Program to deal with some of the basic questions that today's Jews of all ages might ask. In an age of disbelief, how can we affirm our belief in G-d? How can we understand G-d's complex ways? What does G-d expect of us as Jews? And how can Jews find meaning and direction in life today?

The quote from the above prayer, "*Ahavah Rabboh*", mentions "*understanding and insight*" into the Torah before the practice of its laws. It seems that a Jew should have a thorough comprehension of Torah philosophy before he can properly carry out G-d's laws. The more insight one has into His ways, the better he can serve Him.

It is for this reason that we have presented 36 basic questions of Judaism in this work, and have given possible answers to each. These questions have been asked by Jews of all stations, from the beginning student to the most advanced scholar. They are natural queries, ones which all thinking Jews might raise at some time in their life. It is one of the purposes of this book to show that Judaism does not shrink from confronting them.

We advise the reader to read the book from the beginning through to the end and not just pick out chapters at random, since many of the later chapters are based on what was mentioned in the earlier chapters.

All Hebrew words have been transliterated into English and have been italicized. A definition of each Hebrew word has been placed in parentheses right near that word, making it easier for one to understand the word on the spot and not having to look it up in a glossary.

The book, therefore, can be of use to not only the teacher and groupleader, but to the student or layman trying to find meaning to life through Judaism.

Not all possible questions are contained here. Nor are all possible answers given. But is hoped that this work will stimulate thought about life along Torah lines. And we pray that it helps in some small way to clarify the reader's view to life, and increase his appreciation of G-d and Judaism.

Rabbi E. Gevirtz

TABLE OF CONTENTS

PART TWO

PART THREE

PART FOUR

PART FIVE

PART SIX

OVERVIEW:

FAITH AND HASHKOFO

An Overview on Faith and Hashkofo by Rabbi Yisroel Belsky, Mesivta Torah Vodaath

The Talmud in Maseches Makos *(23b) states the following: "Rav Samloi taught: Six hundred thirteen commandments were given to Moshe. Three hundred sixty five prohibitive commandments, equal to the number of days in the solar year, and two hundred forty eight positive commandments, equal to the number of bones in the human body. Then came* Dovid Hamelech *(King David) and based all of these Mitzvos on eleven fundamental principles, (enumerated in Tehillim 15); then came Yeshaya and based them on six principles; then came Michah and based them on three." The Talmud discusses all of these at length and then finally reduces the entire body of Torah law to one basic principle! Thus, "Then came Chababuk and based the entire Torah on one—the righteous one will live by his faith."*

The Rivan (11th-12th century) explains that as each passing generation suffered from the decline of its spiritual level, it became necessary to reduce the field of emphasis, so that those, whose distance from Sinai weakened their power of spirit, might concentrate on fewer areas to achieve what limited success they may. The last and most impoverished generation of all would only be able to focus on one concept—that of faith—and through faith alone, would have to attain the spiritual heights of the previous generations. It is only in our times—as the nation of Israel has become stripped from so much of its former spiritual glory; laid bare to the harsh winds of atheism; decimated by moral decay of which the twentieth century is so fond to identify itself; and bombarded incessantly by the resounding voice of the modern world's valueless nihilism that infiltrates even into our most private quarters through the insidiuous effects of its media—that we have certainly entered into this last phase of decline.

It is manifest that in our times, the battle lines for the survival of Judaism have been drawn along those of faith, with the forces hostile to Torah staking their claims on theories of accidental development and dialectic materialism. Yet, through it all, in defiance of the din and clamor, the steady resistant voice of true faith gains new and potent strength and draws flocks of adherents from within the very bastions of agnosticism who rally to its cause with unbridled enthusiasm. Both the old and the young, intellectuals and pragmatists, often motivated by the bankruptcy of the contemporary faithless society, have recently discovered within the depths of their own souls that ever-present spark of eternity that has been genetically implanted in the Jewish psyche. They have begun to realize truths that have been lost to them with the demise of their grandfathers. Yet strangely, this movement as it were, of the return to faith, has often exhibited a distinct lack of guidance. How often have our hearts been torn asunder by the tragic sight of Jewish children parading before charismatic cultist leaders, demeaning themselves to the dust in the manner of the worshippers of the Baal and the Molech, in a blatant demonstration of the catastrophic effects of misguided faith. Were we to succeed in marshalling all of the Torah world's educational forces and opening before our far flung brethern the portals of the Torah's limitless wisdom, we might channel, with G-d's help, untold members of searching souls—standing on the brink of life's most important decision—into the fold of the Jewish people. For our faith is a faith of wisdom and education. Understanding only strengthens and reinforces the Jewish faith, for our faith has no need for the protective shield of dogma so vital to those other faiths whose main power lies in ignorance.

The opinion has been often expressed that discourses on faith are only for those who have strayed from the truth. A perceptual study of Torah literature shows this to be a highly questionable attitude. Even in times unlike ours, when simple rustic faith might have been adequate for many, the Torah still required of all scholars refinement and development of faith. An adequate treatment of this subject is not within the scope of this article, but the following remarks may suffice.

The Medrash teaches us, "Yisro was only a partial believer, for he had said, 'Now I know that G-d is greater than all deities' " (Shemos 18:11). At face value, Yisro's statement appears to admit to the existence of lesser deities. Yet we know that Yisro was by any standard a great Tzadik who abandoned a life of glory and wealth and followed the divine call into the wilderness for the study of Torah. It is unthinkable to ascribe to Yisro the barest trace of idolatrous thought. What, then, did our sages mean by "partial belief"?

The Rambam, in the opening statement of his monumental work, Yad Hachazokah (Code) writes: *"The foundation of foundations and pillar of all wisdom is the knowledge that there exists a primary being who brought into existence everything that exists . . . This being is G-d . . . Master of the Universe . . . Blessed be He . . . and to know this is a positive commandment as it is written "I am G-d thy G-d" (H. Yesodai Hatorah, Ch. I).*

That this creed is a cornerstone of Jewish belief, a "foundation of foundations", is beyond question. The last portion of the above quotation, however, has puzzled scholars for generations. They ask, how can there be a commandment to believe in G-d when the very idea of a commandment presupposes an already established belief in the existence of the Commander? A great scholar of the last generation, Rabbi Yeruchem Levovitz ZT"L, gave a clear and simple explanation: The knowledge of G-d's existence entails much more than just a simple cut and dried factual acceptance of his being there. It is rather the duty of every Jew to cultivate this acceptance into an awareness, to train himself to sense G-d's existence with every fiber of his body and soul. Dovid Hamelech *(Kind David) said, "I place G-d opposite me at all times." (Teh. 16:8). This means that Dovid Hamelech constantly conditioned his mind to form a perceptive awareness of G-d's presence, not just for one moment of an ecstatic religious "experience", but "at all times"! This is the ultimate goal of the true believer; to expunge from his thoughts any notion of power and being outside of G-d's for even a single moment. A lifetime of work is indeed required to arrive at this lofty level of achievement. Who can truthfully claim that in the presence of a doctor he has never doubted for even a fleeting moment that his cure is entirely in the hands of G-d and that the physician is merely an agent for carrying out His will? Who will say that never, in the conduct of his business affairs, has he contemplated that perhaps, certain measures for improving his lot may have been outside the realm of G-d's management?*

*Thus the commandment to know G-d is addressed specifically to the believer: Know G-d with all of your emotions, become aware of Him, sense His presence in every facet of His wonderful creation, learn to view the entire universe as well as the human microcosm as a reflection of His will! Moshe Rabbeinu had this very same idea in mind when he taught us: "*Veyodata Hayom; *You must know, on this very day, and place firmly into your heart, that G-d is your G-d whose presence is felt in the heavens above and who rules over the earth below, there is nothing else!" (Dev. 4:39).*

Thus there is no longer any difficulty in considering even a righteous man such as Yisro a "partial believer". He had indeed achieved a lofty level of faith in realizing then that "G-d was greater" than all forces and all powers that can be imagined to exist. He was then, no doubt, prepared to embark on the second stage of the development of his faith, to erase from his thoughts the very existence of those powers until he would finally be able to truthfully declare: "There is nothing else!"

The faith of the nation of Israel has been put to various tests throughout the ages. In certain generations, thinkers and philosophers arose who claimed to discover new truths and some of them overwhelmed their contemporary societies with the power of their ideas. Communism and Enlightenment, Aristotlianism and Zoroastianism, to mention just a few, have in their heyday, made such an impact upon the world that those who were not swept along appeared to be outdated and regressive. Great numbers of Jewish people, forever sensitive and open-minded, were swallowed up by these movements, dancing along with religious fervor, becoming their ideologists and leaders, and proclaiming to the rest of the Jewish people that a replacement had finally been found for the Eternal Faith of Israel.

Yet, in every instance, Klal Yisroel *survived the test. We have always been endowed by* Hashem Yisborach, *particularly in times of stress, with leaders and great men who were perceptive enough to recognize the frailty and temporary character of the "modern" philosophies which were soon to become antiquated and outdated by the mere passage of time. They rose to stand at the helm of their people and cured them of their illness by proclaiming to them once again, in contemporary terms, the eternal message of Torah. And so, our literature has become enriched with works such as the* "Emunos Vedaos" *(Beliefs and Ideas) of R. Saadiah Gaon (10th Cent. C.E.),* "Moreh Nevuchem" *(Guide to the Perplexed) of the Rambam (12th Cent.), the* "Sefer Ikrim" *(Book of Principles by R. Yosef Albo (15th Cent.), and the* "Kuzari" *by Rabbi Yehuda Halevi (12th Cent.). At times, the authors of books such as these, chose to use their opponents' own weapons, such as Aristotlian philosophy to prove the falsity of their beliefs and each, in his own manner and by divergent methods, salvaged myriads of Jewish souls from spiritual destruction. Some were severely criticized for what seemed then to be an introduction of harmful elements emanating from alien cultures into Torah.*

In the final analysis, though, the goal of all the authors and their critics has been the same, i.e. to sharpen and cultivate Jewish Faith and to educate the Jewish people with the truth of Torah. Torah never needs apologies written for it, just education! Once the veil of ignorance has been lifted from the face of a Jew, he is well on the way to the final goal, perfection of Faith, the knowledge that "G-d is G-d,—there is nothing else."

Our generation, too, has had its faith put to the test, and as in the past, we have nothing to fear but ignorance. The greatest of our leaders have all told us that we are presently standing on the threshold of the "End of Days", the coming of Moshiach. *The prophet, Yeshaya, said of* Moshiach: *"Faith will gird his loins"* (Yeshaya *11:5) —The power of our Faith will hasten the arrival of* Moshiach. *It is therefore, our task to raise the awareness level of our generation to sense the presence of G-d in every facet of today's technological society, to see within our contemporary concept of nature and the physical world, the reflection of Divine will. Careful thought and discussion will strengthen our faith and belief, not weaken it. The last of the Prophets, Malachi, closed the book on prophecy with a brief discussion concerning the last generation before the "End", the generation that will welcome* Eliyahu Hanovi *and see the return of masses of Jews to the Torah. He wrote:* "At that time those who fear G-d, will discuss things with one another, and G-d will listen closely to their words and record them in a book of remembrance" (Malachi *3:16). We pray that the following discussion will also be included.*

PART ONE

CONSIDERING G-D

SECTION A

PART ONE: CONSIDERING G-D
SECTION A

Question One: *What do we mean by G-d* (Hashem)?

Answer: *"Shema Yisroel Hashem Elokeinu Hashem Echod."*

This familiar quote—"Hear O Israel, *Hashem* is our G-d, *Hashem* is One"— forms the very basis of Jewish belief.

It is said three times daily by Jews throughout the world, as it has been for centuries. It formed the dying words of Jewish martyrs, as they gave their lives to keep their faith. It is a powerful affirmation of the Jews' link to the Almighty.

But who is Hashem?

What do we mean when we refer to G-d?

Is the G-d worshipped by the Jews similar to the mythological deities of the Greeks?

Do we mean the hundreds of divinities of the Hindus, with each god responsible for a different power?

Or should we see G-d as being synonomous with Nature, as the pantheists have claimed?

Not at all.

Judaism does not accept the mythological stories of gods frolicking foolishly in the heavens. It doesn't see G-d as made up of many powerful bits and pieces—for if so, how could He be one all-powerful Being? And it rejects the idea that G-d is simply part of nature, for it believes G-d to be nature's Master.

Instead, Judaism asks man to think of an all-powerful Supreme Being.

It views Him as the Planner, Creator, and Eternal Master of all forces, matter, and life in the cosmos—One Who regulates all existence and gives it meaning.

It sees G-d as an absolute, unlimited Spiritual Being. It believes Him to be everywhere, transcending time, space and nature—knowing all.

And it encourages man to think of Him as a celestial Father. He takes a personal interest in all creatures. He sets objective standards for all men—especially His Chosen People—to live by.

To Jews, G-d is not an imaginary concept, but an ever-present reality. He is Someone to Whom everyone can directly relate. He is the ultimate guardian, Someone to turn to in times of trouble, Someone to express one's deepest feelings to. There is no need for an intermediary when communicating with G-d.

This is what we mean by *Hashem.*

But can we come any closer to the essence of G-d? Can we define Him more specifically, or form a portrait of Him with definite dimensions? Can we point Him out for quick viewing? How do we respond to the assertion of the Russian cosmonaut who said that G-d cannot exist, since he had not seen Him while orbiting the earth?

Why isn't G-d more visible and more easily knowable to man?

To answer this, we must first consider man himself.

Man is, of course, a marvelously complex being. He is an amazing composite of cells that somehow are together capable of great physical feats and outstanding abstract thought. Nevertheless, man is of limited capacity. He may think of himself as gigantic when compared to an amoeba, but he is dwarfed by a tall mountain; and, strong as he is, he cannot move that mountain by himself. Left entirely without aid, he cannot fly like a bird, or produce food like a plant; and without oxygen, food, and water, he will die.

His ability to think also has its limits. The average person may be able to do certain mathematical problems, but he will probably fail when asked to multiply two 50-digit numbers within a matter of seconds, without any outside help. His limited senses enable him to comprehend only a limited number of sensations and dimensions. No man can truly claim to know everything that is happening today or accurately predict everything that will occur tomorrow.

Man is not a superman. The human body, though extremely supple, is comprised of a limited number of cells which eventually deteriorate and die. Likewise, the human brain, though incredibly adept, operates under limited patterns defined by set electrical and chemical reactions.

Therefore, when we discuss the essence of G-d, we are faced with a major problem. We are forced to use our limited mental capacity to try to comprehend a boundless, omnipotent force.

This is not fully possible. It is like expecting a fly to use its "brain" to solve an algebraic problem or to understand human psychology. These phenomena are beyond the fly's dimensions of comprehension. Similary, G-d is dimensions beyond what man can understand. Man has enough trouble grappling with concepts like infinity and relativity. How can he then hope to fully comprehend the G-d who is responsible for them? Even Moshe Rabbeinu, whose Jewish spiritual intellect was supreme, was not capable of total insight into G-d and His ways. If we cannot grasp all aspects of G-d, it is because of man's limitations, not G-d's.

Therefore, it is absurd to say that G-d does not exist because He cannot be seen. Only physical entities can be seen through man's limited vision, and G-d is not a physical being. If G-d had a fixed physical form, it would limit Him, and He would not be a boundless, omnipotent Deity.

G-d then, cannot be seen or touched. Still, that does not mean that He is not present. We can neither see love nor touch hate, but love and hate certainly exist in the world. We cannot hold on to an isolated electric current, or put it into a dish with our bare hands. Nevertheless, we can see the effects of such a current, such as the heat and the light it can produce. In that way, we know that it exists. In this same way, we can prove G-d's existence through His manifestations—His worldly creations, His guiding of history—even if we cannot see G-d Himself.

Further insight into the ways and nature of G-d come from His holy communication to man: His Torah. The Torah's many references to G-d's supposed physical attributes—telling of His "outstretched arm" or His emotions—may seem puzzling. As we just mentioned, G-d is limitless, so He cannot have a body. Rather, say our Rabbonim, the Torah describes G-d in physical terms to make G-d more understandable to man. In this way, man can form at least a limited concept of G-d within man's own level of understanding. (In the same way, we describe inanimate forces in human terms — "Mother Nature," "Father Time"— to make them more comprehensible to children.) And from the Torah's discussion of G-d's "characteristics" and "feelings," man can take a hint as to how G-d wants him to behave. If G-d is described as being modest, kindly, and forgiving, these are attributes He seeks in man.

It is in this sense that man is created "in G-d's image," as the Torah states. The notion that man looks exactly like G-d can't be correct, for G-d has no body. Rather, say our Sages, man resembles G-d in a spiritual sense. Man is endowed with free will, with the ability to tell right from wrong, to be kind or callous. Plants or animals don't have a choice of how to behave; man does. It is up to man to behave righteously. If he does, he can begin to have some notion of G-d's essence.

Question Two: How can one go about proving the existence of G-d?

Answer: Proving that G-d exists is hardly a commonplace process. It is not quite the same as proving the existence of something like bacteria. After all, one can use a microscope to actually see the bacteria, and then one can be sure that they are there.

G-d, on the other hand, is not a physical entity. He cannot be hauled into a scientist's laboratory and be studied under a microscope or a spotlight. G-d transcends the laws of time and space, and thus the scientific method cannot be used to prove His existence. If G-d is not fully knowable to man, as we mentioned earlier, then how can man demonstrate that the unknowable is a known fact?

Yet, while the direct proof of G-d may be beyond man's abilities, an indirect approach is certainly possible. Let us deal with what we can observe—the world around us. We can examine its contents, its inhabitants, its natural laws, and its history. All these leave implications for the existence of a Supreme Being, which we call G-d.

In short, the indirect proof can work as follows: Suppose we see a 50-story skyscraper, which dazzles us with its complexity. We note that each brick, each window, has been put in its proper, functional place; that each floor is constructed so that it is roomy enough for offices in which work takes place; that the wiring and plumbing work satisfactorily; and that the roof is so constructed that it does not cave in. We would then say without hesitation that the building must have been carefully designed by an architect and put together by a construction team. No one would claim that the bricks and windows somehow fell together at random and just happened to form a building fit for human use. That would be too absurd to even consider. No—the building must have been deliberately planned and constructed by those with the physical and intellectual ability to do so.

The world is certainly bigger and more complex than a single building. Yet, as we will soon see, it exhibits the same careful design, the same orderliness, the same purposeful accomodations that a skyscraper does. Consequently, we must conclude that it, too, was planned, designed, and created by a Supreme Architect. This is G-d.

We will soon discuss this and other proofs in detail. They, too, are based on the unlikelihood that the complexity of life is totally accidental. Something as intricate as man must have had a Creator.

Nevertheless, there are always those who reject this evidence. "We won't accept G-d until we see Him directly," they say. They maintain this attitude even though G-d is not a viewable Being, as we mentioned earlier.

Ultimately, then, accepting G-d's existence is a matter of belief. Some will insist that they do not believe in G-d. But others feel that everything about life, the world, and the cosmos, strengthens their belief that there is, indeed, a G-d.

We will soon see why.

Question Three: Does it make a difference whether or not we believe in G-d?

Answer: To deal with this question, let us first view the universe through the eyes of a non-believer—one who sees everything as a result of some primordial accident rather than a planned Creation.

This individual will have to say that no Being designed the earth or its inhabitants, no one caused their emergence, and no one is guiding them now. Instead, he will be faced with the conclusion that the world is a free-floating orb suspended senselessly in space, full of occupants who have no particular business being there. There is no purpose or reason for the existence of anything. Whatever is, came about by accident. All of life is, therefore, absurd and meaningless, without direction or purpose; and nothing that happens makes any difference in the long run.

Some embrace this philosophy with glee. They feel that it gives them a sense of freedom. With no G-d and no Torah to obey, they feel they do not have to adhere to any fixed moral laws. They assert that they can rise above the outdated bonds of tradition and can assume a modern, sophisticated view of life. They say they no longer have to fear Divine punishment—and, therefore, they will have fewer compunctions about sinning. They might see themselves as having grown up, and no longer having to worry about a Divine Father watching their every move.

However, they can also be viewed as children removing themselves from their parents' guardianship. This can create problems. The child without parental supervision can fail to develop self-discipline. He may be tempted to abuse his freedom at the expense of others. If he starts shoplifting or vandalizing public property, what is to stop him?

Similarly, one who denies G-d can also deny the existence of objective moral laws. Suppose the human criminal justice system proves ineffective, and criminals go uncaught. One who denies the existence of a watchful G-d might try to take advantage. With no one to see the wrong he's doing—with no one to make him accountable for his acts—he might lose all self-control in getting everything he wants.

Of course, it would be wrong to list all atheists as probable criminals. Even those who don't believe in G-d might want to behave ethically, either because they want to avoid negative repercusssions, or simply because they think it is right. Nevertheless, their lives may have a certain emptiness at the core. They may be nagged by a gnawing doubt: If the world is a freak of nature, then life has no purpose. It is a meaningless absurdity. If so, what difference does their existence make? After all, not only they, but all that they accomplished will soon crumble into dust. So what good is happiness if it will soon disappear? What good are artistic creations, or scientific discoveries? They're only temporary achievements in a temporary existence, so why bother? In fact, why bother living at all?

Now let's take the opposing view: That a Divine Being created the world with a purpose and a plan, and provided man with basic laws of right and wrong. Then life is no longer an accident, but something carefully designed. Man is no longer something that just happened to come about, but a deliberately crafted creature with a G-d-given mission in life: to bring G-dly righteousness to the world. The world is no longer absurd, but a sensible creation.

Now life takes on meaning; now existence is long-lasting; now man becomes important, and his actions make a difference. Man becomes a jewel in a carefully-designed setting, rather than a bit of dross dropped at random. If he brings happiness to others, if he creates something worthwhile, he has had an effect, because he has enhanced a meaningful world, and has met G-d's standards. Similarly, the believer has a reason to act ethically at all times, even when he knows no human court will try him. For he is aware that though he might escape man's justice, he cannot evade the final judgment of G-d, Who sees all. One who truly accepts G-d has clear-cut moral laws on which to base his behavior. He will abide by these rules no matter what. It is he who has developed real self-discipline. He can withstand negative temptation—and in this sense, he is the one who is really free.

In short, then, whether one accepts or rejects G-d's presence can have a profound influence on his life-view and his actions. If one says that there is no G-d, then he admits there is no all-seeing Regulator of the world—and he invites the conclusion that life is absurd. But if one accepts G-d's existence, he has the comfort of knowing that his positive actions will be recognized, and that his moral acts will bear fruit, for G-d stands behind him. The world makes sense, and life has meaning.

Question Four: How do we know that G-d created the world and its living inhabitants?

Answer: Let us begin by recognizing the fact that the world exists. This immediately leads to a question: How did the earth come into being?

Both the Torah and the scientific world agree that the earth did not always exist in its present form. Its physical features indicate that it has existed for a set period of time—not forever. Therefore, at some point in time, it must have come into being.

However, our observations also indicate that everything that comes into being must be derived from something else. Nothing we know of can spring into existence from absolutely nothing. True, matter can be converted into energy and vice versa. But no one has ever seen either matter or energy emerge entirely by themselves. The theory of spontaneous generation has long been discredited.

This just reinforced our previous question. When, then, did our earth—or for that matter, our universe, or our galaxy—come from? How did it get to be what it is today?

Scientists have developed several different theories about this over the years. They weren't around in person to witness the universe's debut, of course, so they have to resort to educated guesses—educated perhaps; but guesses, nonetheless.

One very popular theory about the origins of the earth was recently summmarized as follows: "Most cosmologists believe that the universe is the expanding remnant of a huge fireball that was created 20 billion years ago by the explosion of a giant primordial atom—the 'big bang theory.' "

According to this view, the solar system is the remnant of a giant mass that exploded very long ago. This may seem reasonable, but it just brings us back to our original question. This mass was apparently great enough to supply our solar system with huge quantities of matter and energy. *But where did this primordial mass come from?* According to natural law, nothing comes from nothing. We still have our question: What produced the original matter and energy?

A problem.

Yet, it need not be so, if we accept the Torah's position that the original matter was brought into being from nothing *(creation ex nihilo)* by a Supreme Creator.

In short, G-d created the earth and the entire universe from nothing. Only G-d can do this, because He is all-powerful, and is not limited by the domain of science and natural laws—after all, He created that too. How exactly G-d was able to accomplish this creation is not knowable to man. However, man can know the basic fact that everything was created by a Superior Builder, rather than somehow bursting forth into existence on its own.

Some will ask a very natural question here: "But where did G-d come from? Who created G-d?"

This is not an obstacle. It is true that all physical matter must be derived from something already in existence, but G-d is, by definition, limitless. G-d has no physical properties. He is beyond the laws of nature, since He preceded and formulated nature. Therefore, he transcends the natural laws of creation. He originated time, and therefore, existed before the start of time. Consequently, G-d had no beginning, and has no end. He has always been, and will always be. He needed no creator, for if He did, He would not be G-d.

We have, then, two alternative views of how the world came about. Either we can believe that all matter emerged spontaneously, without any creator—though there is no explanation of how this phenomenon could have happened. Or we can believe that G-d (Who transcends the laws of nature and Who exists forever) created the original matter. The second approach provides a reasonable interpretation of how matter originated, while the first leaves the question dangling.

So far we have been dealing with the beginnings of the universe, an event man obviously could not witness. Let us, therefore, turn to something we can indeed see—the world around us. This includes natural matter, living organisms, and the processes of nature. An investigation of all of these can strengthen our belief that G-d created them.

As we mentioned earlier, the more orderly something is, the less likely it is that it came about by accident. No one would claim that the "Mona Lisa" was formed by an accidental spill of paint. How could such a well-ordered piece of work have been formed by mere chance? How could the paint know where to go to form the model's eyes, nose and unique smile? What are the odds against all the different colors settling in the exact proper places? Astronomical, to say the least.

No one would argue the fact that the "Mona Lisa" was created with purposeful care by an artist—as no one would debate the fact that the Mount Rushmore sculptures were chiseled by a sculptor rather than by the erosion of rock. Such results do not come from chance occurrences.

In spite of this, some of those who would accept these statements as truth would still claim that the world is an accident of history. They agree that someone created the "Mona Lisa"—but they deny that someone created the world. And this, despite the fact that when one stops to consider it, the world is just as well-ordered and carefully organized as any painting—and much more complex.

What do we mean by this? The following will provide some specific illustrations.

A. **Natural Laws.** Do you know what time the sun will rise tomorrow? Can you predict when summer will begin? Do you know in which direction an object will go when you release it from the ceiling of a room?

The answer to all of these is, of course, yes.

This is because the earth's movements and forces remain constant, and therefore, predictable. Natural law prompts the earth to circle the sun according to a set pattern. In other words, there is a predictable order to the way in which even inanimate things like the earth act. The order is a perfectly logical one—a pattern that enables the earth to support life.

Consider the rain cycle, as charted by scientists. The sun causes water vapor to arise from the seas, in accordance with the natural law that heat causes matter to expand, and that less dense matter rises above denser material. This vapor accumulates in clouds, which the wind disperses over the earth. The clouds give off the condensed vapor, and the pull of gravity causes the rain to fall. It also makes sure that excess rain flows to the seas. Then the cycle begins all over again.

Notice the intricate order of the cycle, and all the laws of nature that must operate in order for it to work. And consider how each item—the sun, the sea, the clouds, the wind, the gravity—is essential to the continuation of the cycle. If anything were missing—if the sun were too weak to evaporate the water, or if the wind did not blow the clouds but rather let them accumulate only over bodies of water—the cycle could not function properly. All parts of the cycle fit together with incredible precision. And the cycle is absolutely essential for the proper maintenance of life, for without rain, plants would not grow, and animals and man would have no source of food, water, or oxygen.

Only a Divine Being could have planned such a complex and vital process so meticulously.

Similarly, the nitrogen cycle makes sure that nitrogenous wastes produced by living organisms are decomposed and passed back into the atmosphere. It also sees to it that nitrogen in the atmosphere is converted into nitrates that are essential for plants to survive. For this cycle to function, there must be sufficient nitrogen in the atmosphere, as well as nitrifying, denitrifying, and nitrogen-fixing bacteria—all of which play important parts in the cycle. If any of these is missing, the cycle could not proceed, and life would be disrupted. Yet, the cycle continues like clockwork—because Someone built the 'clock' and keeps it 'ticking.' If this weren't the case, how could such inanimate forces have come to operate so efficiently and so purposefully?

Note that all these processes of nature are not only complex and well-ordered, but also necessary for the maintenance of living things. Without the rain, and without the nitrogen cycle, plants could not flourish, and animals would lack food. Without gravity, living beings would float off into space. If the earth did not orbit around the sun in a systematic way, chaos would result. If the earth were any closer to the sun, all living things would be burned to a crisp. If it were any farther away, all matter would freeze. The mere existence of these cycles and laws indicates that the world was deliberately positioned and established in a way that would allow life to flourish upon it. In short, natural laws seem to have been designed with the purpose of sustaining life.

Let us look at another example. Consider the fact that the colder water becomes, the heavier it gets. Yet, somehow, when water is cooled to 4 degrees centigrade, it suddenly becomes lighter. This reversal of natural law would seem to be senseless. But, because of it, when water freezes in a pond or lake, ice forms on the top rather than at the bottom, because it is less dense. Consequently, fish at the bottom are able to continue living, rather than freezing to death. It seems that even the laws of nature are themselves suspended at times in order to facilitate life. (Similarly, plants are able to turn upwards towards the light, even though this goes against the laws of gravity; otherwise, the plants would wither away.)

What do the above illustrations show? Firstly, that the laws of nature operate in a systematic way, as if someone had designed them; and secondly, that these laws serve to maintain life, as if someone had instituted them with that purpose. Nature seems to know exactly what it is doing, and why.

But what is nature, anyway? There is no Mother Nature guiding the seasons and the cycles with a magic wand. Science tells us only *how* nature operates, not *why*. Actually then, how did the laws of nature originate? Did the planets suddenly conspire to institute the laws of gravity? Did the clouds and the sun join forces out of boredom to initiate rain? Did water decide to rebel against nature to preserve the fish population? Are all these processes freak accidents? And if so, how did they come to operate so well? How did they manage to promote life so ably?

Or do they show that a Divine Creator planned and instituted the laws of nature in order to maintain and benefit His living creations?

Judaism opts for the latter view.

B. **Living Organisms.** Now let's turn to a study of living things.

If we marvel at the majestic ways of nature, we must be awe-struck by the intricacies of animate beings.

Take man, for instance. His development alone is incredible almost beyond belief.

If someone gave you a crumb of cake and told you to stock a

bakery shop with it, you'd think he was crazy. How could anyone possibly begin with a speck of pastry and watch it develop into a whole cake, icing and all?

Certainly man is more complex than a cake. Yet, he begins life as nothing more than a microscopic cell—a zygote, formed by the uniting of two other miniscule cells, the sperm and the egg. From this tiny speck of matter emerges a being composed of thousands upon thousands of cells. Incredible!

Yet not only are the cells numerous, they are also amazingly functional. Somehow, each group of cells seems to know what job it must do to make the whole organism work. The nerve cells must convey sensations and respond to dangers. The cardiac cells must keep the heart beating so blood can be pumped throughout the body. Other cells must fight germs, or digest food, or aid in reproduction. Glands must secrete enzymes to produce proper growth and maintain proper equilibrium in the body. The respiratory system must carry oxygen to the cells and remove carbon dioxide from the body. The digestive system must break down foods and make them usable for the organism. The most intricate electrical and chemical processes occur regularly, to keep the body functioning as it was meant to.

What should be especially kept in mind is how the various cells and organs must work together to keep the organism alive. If one of the body's systems malfunctions—if the lungs or the heart or the brain stops working—the whole operation stops functioning. The systems either work together, or they don't work at all.

The assembly line efficiency of the human body existed long before factories began operating. Could anyone say that all the cogs of all the machines in a factory were dropped haphazardly around, until they began operating in unison? Of course not. The machines we use today are carefully designed so that they will be usable; engineers spend long hours figuring out how to construct them. Once the various machines are built, more painstaking planning is needed to determine how they can be operated together to produce the desired product.

Somehow, the myriad of differentiated cells in a human body operate in such harmony that they form a walking, talking, seeing, loving and thinking human being.

Who can say that a Supreme Engineer did not design such a wondrous creature?

Furthermore, if we examine the different parts of the human body, who can deny that they are at least as complex as the most intricate machines? In fact, many machines are based on their human counterparts. The camera wasn't developed until the 19th century, but the human eye functioned like a camera long before that. We may take sight for granted, but we wouldn't if we considered the various components of the eye that make it possible: the pupil, acting as the shutter letting in light; the lens, allowing the light to focus properly on the retina, which in turn relays the message of what is seen to the brain via the optic nerve; the rods and cones, which account for color and black and white vision; the cornea, which protects the eye from damage; the tear ducts, which help remove foreign substances from it—not to mention the fact that the brain receives the image upside down, and must turn it right side up before the image registers. All of these parts and operations occur so that man will be able to see and appreciate the world around him. A blind man fully realizes what he is missing by not having sight. Could such an incredible process—reproducing a physical object within a minor part of the brain, by means of so many specialized parts—have originated without having been designed?

The same, of course, is true of the processes of hearing, smelling, tasting, touching, eating, growing, and breathing, among others. These operations all require the use of specialized, intricate organs that are equivalent to the most sophisticated tools. And they work on the basis of chemical and physical reactions that can be copied—if at all—only in the most sophisticated of laboratories. Man didn't know about the wonders of electricity until fairly recently—yet his reflexes operated through electric currents from the day he first walked the earth. Did electricity join the human body by total chance?

Perhaps the most incredible of all is the human brain—an object so intricate that it has not yet been able to figure itself out. It is only a grayish jelly-like piece of matter, yet not only can it regulate the human body's actions, it can also cause him to have emotions, appreciate art, think abstractly, and gain insight. How can a tangible piece of matter produce intangible thoughts and feelings? How can billions of neurons cooperate so efficiently? No one knows, but they *do*. That remains a testimonial to the fact that this must have been formed by a Superior Being and a Master Chemist. Maybe G-d made the human brain so special because it is the only earthly matter that can conceive of Him.

We have gone into some detail to show how man's features are so complex and so well coordinated that they must have beer planned by a Superior Being. Obviously, this Deity wanted man to function on the earth that He had created. And, barring any physical damage, man can function quite well. Not only do the various systems of his body work in unison, but he has built-in features that can prevent malfunctions. For instance, man takes in air and food through the same opening—the mouth. The air must go through one pipe in his throat, while the food goes through another. If there is a mix-up here, death can result. So the body has a built-in muscle that can cover the wind pipe while the food pipe is being used, and vice versa. And if someone talks while he is eating, and the food goes down the wrong pipe, the body's natural reaction is to automatically cough up the food, to further prevent harm. Similarly, if dangerous particles enter the body, they can be expelled through sneezing or coughing. If they aren't, the body can still fight them by means of automatically-produced antibodies. Likewise, if someone senses danger from without, his body spontaneously produces adrenalin, which increases his heartbeart, so that he has extra energy with which to escape.

These safety devices do not always work, of course; death sometimes occurs. G-d can decide to let them operate properly or—possibly as punishment—not to. Those who abuse their G-d-given bodies will be more likely to see the body misfunction sooner. But these built-in life saving features indicate that life is worth preserving. No one would bother protecting an object if he didn't feel it was important. The fact that man is protected with these "life preservers" indicates that his Creator felt he was worth keeping alive. Man—and life—must be important.

The same complex life-preserving instincts are found in the animal world. Many animals have shapes or colors that camouflage them, so that they will not be eaten by predators. The snowshoe rabbit, for instance, is white in the winter, and brown in the summer. This allows it to blend in with the snow in the winter and the vegetation in the summer, so that other animals won't be able to find it. Many insects and reptiles resemble twigs or leaves and can therefore not be detected when in trees. This way, the animals can stay alive. Are these accidents—or planned phenomena?

Consider also the way animals build nests for their unborn progeny, or the way they store food for the winter, or the way baby chicks peck their way out of egg shells. Certainly, these organisms don't "know" exactly what they're doing. They don't have the intellectual ability to reason or think. If a spider is stopped in mid-web, it will not have the insight to be able to continue where it left off, but will have to start all over again. Similarly, animals don't read Dr. Spock to learn how to raise their offspring; nevertheless, they know exactly how to provide them with their basic needs. This is because animals have been blessed with set instinctual reactions that keep them and their offspring alive. How did these reactions appear? Did they occur by mere chance? Or were they implanted into the animals' genetic composition to assure them the opportunity of staying alive and fulfilling their purpose on earth? And if they were implanted, by whom was this done?

(The fact that some species have become extinct is not a problem. Man has the free will to act as he wants, as we will discuss later, and he bears the blame for making some of G-d's creatures extinct. Other species may have been removed from the earth because G-d may have felt that their mission in life had been completed.)

Plants also have this built-in tendency to survive. The plant's stem will automatically grow towards the sun, so that photosynthesis can occur. On the other hand, the roots will grow down towards water. Sunshine and water are essential to the plant's ability to produce food. How did these automatic tropisms come about? Were they accidental, or purposeful?

Not only does the individual seem to be programmed to stay alive, but also the entire species. Reproduction is a basic life function. All species must reproduce to carry on, and all do, even though the individual might have nothing to gain by reproducing.

Some methods of reproduction are truly remarkable. For fruit-bearing plants to reproduce, their seeds must be carried to a suitable planting spot. These seeds are therefore contained inside fruits. When a person or an animal detaches a fruit, eats it, and throws the pit onto the ground, a new plant is able to germinate. It hardly seems a coincidence, then, that most fruits are both colorful and tasty. This way, they can attract those who eat the fruits and deposit the seeds. On the other hand, fruits that are not yet ready for this process (or foods like the potato, which must be further prepared before being eaten) are unattractively green or brown—signs that they are unripe and shouldn't be eaten yet. This means that their seeds will not be spread prematurely—and also helps men and animals avoid a stomach ache by not eating them.

Consider also how watermelon seeds are small and can easily be swallowed. Is it an accident that they are also slippery, which helps make sure that they are often dropped to the soil rather than swallowed? On the other hand, the orange seed is not tasty, and there is little chance that it will be swallowed. Instead, it will be deliberately thrown to the ground. Is it any wonder, then, that it is *not* slippery?

Animals and humans reproduce sexually. The strong natural tendency associated with this process guarantees that even those who know nothing about biology will tend to mate. This guarantees that these species, and especially man, will not disappear from the earth under normal circumstances. After all, G-d has created them to "be fruitful and multiply", to perform their role in the life process.

Now consider the fact that when humans, animals, plants, and even one-celled organisms reproduce, they create almost exact copies of themselves. A cow does not give birth to a dog; a tree will produce another tree. If this weren't true, chaos would result. The world would have to be redesigned to accomodate every new generation of freaks.

We are only now just beginning to understand the intricacies involved in making this so. In higher forms of life, the traits of the parents are transmitted by chromosomes, themselves, composed of intricate substances like DNA and RNA. In the case of man, each cell normally has 46 chromosomes. Before reproduction occurs, the egg and sperm cells—and only these cells—undergo a process called meiosis. Miraculously, the chromosomes divide, so that each egg and sperm cell has only 23 chromosomes. That way, when the egg and sperm unite, the resulting zygote will again have 46 chromosomes, and can develop into a human with traits like those of its parents. These cells don't "know" that they must act this way. Yet, they do, because they have been programmed to—thus allowing life to continue generation after generation without major hitches. (This basic constancy in each species—and therefore, in the earth's history—helps make the Torah timeless for all generations.)

Man, despite his superior intelligence, has not yet been able to create a single living human cell. Certainly, such a cell has not developed by mere chance. Yet, the miracle of childbirth takes place countless times daily. Could this process have originated by accident?

Reproduction makes sure that life—in all its complexity—goes on and on. If life has meaning, this makes sense. If life is an accident, it does not.

Let's go on. The world does not consist of separate creatures living in isolation from each other. For the earth to be a workable entity, its living inhabitants must interact. Otherwise, there would be no reason to have them all living in the same place at the same time. So consider how living things are interdependent. Scientists speak of an ecologically balanced community of organisms. This means that practically all members of the community are needed for all of them to benefit. This is true, by and large, of the entire world community.

For instance, there are countless plants in the world. Why are they necessary? What can they contribute to the rest of the world? For one thing, they are the only organisms that produce their own food. As a result, they are essential links in the universal food chain. Both man and animals rely on plants for food as well as oxygen. Furthermore, they provide man with raw materials (for paper, rubber, etc.) shade, and beauty. At the same time, man and animals return the favor by helping spread plant seeds.

In a similar way, animals—both large and small—provide man

with food, milk, skins, labor, and companionship. By studying how animals function, man can learn more about how his own body works to fight disease and reproduce genetically (which may be one reason why G-d created animal bodies functionally similar to man's). Even insects sometimes help man, for bees produce honey and spread pollen, and others help remove unwanted wastes. (Harmful insects and animals can serve as an instrument of G-d to punish man when necessary.) Conversely, man can help animals survive by caring for them and providing them with food.

In short, each general species seems to have its own role in ensuring that the world functions properly, and that other species can continue to survive. It is as if the earth were a party to which only important and needed guests came. Did the guests wander in entirely on their own? *Or were they specifically invited by the One who arranged the "party," G-d?*

Finally, consider man's place in the world. It seems as if he is the only one who can make full use of all the other creations. Only man can truly harness the world's natural resources. Animals can make little use of coal, oil, electricity, metals, sound waves, or most minerals—but man has used them to provide heat, tools, building material, and methods of communication. Animals have no need for such creations as cotton, wheat, or rubber. Yet, they exist, and man has put them to good use. Without man being here, these aspects of the world would have absolutely no purpose. So it seems that the world was designed specifically with man in mind. It is perhaps for this reason that man was created last, according to the Torah. G-d served the world to him on a ready-made platter. All other creations help man survive.

Why, then, was man created? The Torah says that he was created in G-d's image. He is G-d's representative on earth, and as such can carry out G-d's righteousness and good will on this world. G-d was careful to provide man with free will. Unlike the animals, which act only on the basis of unquestioning instinct and without any alternatives, man has freedom of choice. He is the unpredictable variable on this world that can either maintain the G-d-created balance among all living things, or can upset it through his mistakes. Man can, by working in harmony with others, set up a paradise on earth. Or, by giving in to his baser tendencies towards self-obsession and deceit, he can lead the world to the brink of destruction.

G-d's Torah clearly outlines the Jew's purpose on earth, and indicates what *all* men should accomplish: to freely choose right over wrong and good over bad, so that all men can benefit as a result. Man is the only creation that can make this choice: man is the only creation that can appreciate his Creator. And only by realizing that he is a creation of G-d, and that G-d gave him a mission in life, can man use his life for the purpose it was meant. That is why these proofs of G-d's existence are so important for man to consider.

To sum up then: Many factors argue for the existence of a Supreme Being, called G-d, Who actively created the world and its inhabitants. These include:

a) The presence of matter, energy, natural laws, and living organisms, which could not have sprouted from nothingness unless a Creator formed them.

b) The logical intricacies of the laws of nature which help maintain life, indicating they were deliberately planned by a Creator.

c) The complexity of living things, showing that they could not have come about by accident.

d) The complex ways in which living organisms and nature operate, and the methods in which they tend to cling to life, implying that life is meaningful and purposeful.

e) The close interaction among living organisms, and between animate and inanimate objects, showing that each species on earth has a purpose—as if the world were a successful jigsaw puzzle put together by a Superior Intellect.

f) The appearance of man, who can make full use of the world's other features and resources, and who can comprehend G-d's hopes for him, indicating that G-d created the world with him in mind.

We began this section with two alternatives. One held that the world came about totally by accident, and had no purpose in forming. *The other held that the world was created by G-d, who carefully planned its formation and gave meaning to its existence.*

The first alternative relies mostly on wishful thinking for those who refuse to believe in G-d. *The second one is backed by the reasons mentioned above.* ***For believers, all aspects of the world around us point to G-d being behind it.***

CONSIDERING G-D

SECTION B

CONSIDERING G-D
SECTION B

Q*uestion Five: Why can't the development of life be explained by the Theory of Evolution instead?*

A*nswer:* The Theory of Evolution revolutionized modern thought. From the time of ancient Rome until the mid-19th century, the Western world generally believed that man was a creation of G-d. The Theory of Evolution then presented an alternative to this belief, one which has gained wide acceptance.

What is the Theory of Evolution?

Essentially, it claims that all life developed on its own, without the aid of a Creator. According to the theory, after the first one-celled organisms spontaneously appeared, new and more complex species evolved from them, through subtle changes. Evolutionists have changed their opinion on how these changes occurred. At first, they believed they were caused by the inheritance of acquired characteristics; now they say they are due to genetic mutations. The organisms with beneficial new features survived at the expense of organisms without them, in a process termed "survival of the fittest." They passed down new features to their offspring; and this process continued until increasingly complex forms of life—including man—came about. The evolutionists say that this process has been going on for a very long time—millions of years—and that all species with their unique features developed entirely by chance.

Evolutionists offer the following arguments as evidence for their claims: a) Archaeologists have unearthed fossils they claim are millions of years old, supporting the contention that life has existed for a very long time. b) Furthermore, fossils found in rock strata usually show the simpler organisms located below more complex ones. This, they say, shows that more complex organisms evolved from simpler ones. c) Some fossils seem to be early forms of man, indicating that man and the ape are branches of the same common stem. d) Mutations in species (such as the appearances of insects with resistance to DDT) have been observed, and these newly acquired features have been inherited by succeeding generations. e) Man has what are termed vestigial organs which have no apparent purpose (like the appendix), and which must, therefore, have been retained from earlier species during the evolutionary process.

Acceptance of the evolutionary theory among most (but not all) scientists sometimes makes one overlook the many problems with it. These include the following:

1) **Remember that the** concept of development by evolution is only a theory. No scientist was present when life first appeared. No scientist has ever observed the evolution of a single new species! No one can prove beyond a doubt that all living organisms developed by means of an evolutionary process. The theory has even been changed several times over the years (relying first on the assumption of acquired characteristics and then on mutations, for instance), because parts of it have been disproved. Yet, many scientists, have come to accept it with an astonishing religiosity, and denounce anyone who questions the theory as an old-fashioned, narrow-minded heretic. Is this true scientific objectivity?

2) **The Theory of Evolution** rejects the idea of a Divine Creator (meaning, incidentally, that it embraces the idea that life is absurd, as we mentioned earlier.) Consequently, evolutionists must explain the development of all animate and inanimate objects as being the result of pure chance. They must say that all of the steps that led from the appearance of the first one-celled organism to that of man came about purely by accident. Every single organ, limb, brain cell, and artistic and emotional aspect of man resulted from a series of coincidences.

But we have already discussed the incredible intricacy of not only man, but also other living creatures. We have shown how harmoniously the different species work together to produce a viable earthly community, and how the laws of nature aid in maintaining life. Can all of this have been the consequence of trial and error—of a world trying over and over again to make something of itself, and then suddenly hitting the jackpot?
Consider the odds against a blindfolded person picking out letters at random and finding that, when put in the order he has chosen

them, they form a perfectly logical novel! No matter how many times he would try the stunt, he would undoubtedly fail. A novel is nothing when compared to the world itself. As vast as it is, the earth makes sense. It is a giant jigsaw puzzle whose pieces fit together with amazing precision. Could the pieces have been placed together at random?

Evolutionists say that man evolved from a one-celled organism, purely by chance. Yet it has been calculated that the probability of forming a single protein molecule by chance is one in 10^{243} (10 with 242 zeroes behind it.) Furthermore, even if the world were covered by an ocean a mile deep containing 10^{33} bacteria, scientists say it would take more than 100 *billion* years for them to produce a single new enzyme. And even if they produced a gene to manufacture this new enzyme, six million generations would have to elapse for the gene to spread throughout the species by the process of survival of the fittest. The above is the time needed to develop a typical *non-useful* enzyme. For a single useful enzyme to appear, it would take *three hundred million years! (A Torah and Science Reader,* p. 29) This points out the improbability that even one-celled fully functional organisms developed by pure chance. If so many chance occurrences and so much time were needed to form just a single useful enzyme, imagine how many coincidences and how many eons would be required for the one cell to evolve into billion-celled man! No one could possibly calculate the odds against this happening by chance. Yet, the evolutionists ask us to swallow this whole.

3) **The evolutionists, who** deny a Creator, must explain where the original matter came from. The earth, the moon, the sun, the stars—all are gigantic bodies, operating exquisitely under natural laws. How did they get there? How did atoms originate and elements start? How did the laws of nature begin? There is no solution to this in evolution.

Evolutionists must also explain how the first living cell came into being. We know that living cells, like matter and energy, do not pop out of thin air: Pasteur showed that spontaneous generation (life emerging spontaneously) cannot occur. Yet, evolutionists are forced to say that the first cells did appear by means of spontaneous generation. But if so, why have scientists, with all their advanced know-how, been unable to create one single living cell? (True, they have been able to manufacture amino acids and viruses, but these are not true living cells. And even if a living cell had somehow miraculously formed out of the elements and gases available on the earth, it would have been killed by ultraviolet rays from the sun—unless, of course, a G-d created and protected it.)

Furthermore, how could these first cells have attained their life-preserving traits, like respiration and ingestion? How—and why—did they begin reproducing? What prompted them to behave as if life was worth preserving?

4) **Basic to the theory** of evolution is the idea that the changes that enabled an amoeba to change into man resulted from mutations. Originally, Charles Darwin, the father of the theory, assumed that these new characteristics were slowly acquired and passed down to the organisms' offspring. For instance, he believed that if a giraffe had an unusually long neck due to extensive reaching for food, it passed down this superior trait to its young, and the long- necked giraffes eventually out-survived those with shorter necks since they had better access to food on trees. But there were major problems with this idea. For one thing, the acquired traits were not inherited by the young; for another, such a process would take an extremely long time. So a new idea was substituted. The changes came about through sudden, major changes in the genes, and in this way were passed down to the next generation.

This might seem plausible, especially since mutations have been observed, as we mentioned earlier. However, problems still remain. While mutations can occur, they have not yet produced one new type of limb or organ in any species. New DDT-resistant insects and black-colored moths have been produced through mutations—but these are still the same essential insects and moths. In fact, most mutations are extremely harmful to the organism. Mutations in the fruit fly caused wings that were smaller and crumpled, but none that were larger or stronger. Mutations among animals resulted in weaker and shorter specimens: those among plants caused seedless varieties. And in man, x-rays have caused mutations that produced cancer, idiocy, sickle-cell anemia, hemophilia, and lack of tooth enamel. No one has ever observed mutations making one class of animal into a more complex type of organism.

How then, can evolutionists confidently claim that every step up the long, long ladder from the amoeba to man was caused by mutations? How can they say that mutations made new organisms more fit to survive?

Man and one-celled organisms are so different that it seems incredible that one developed into the other. Even the differences between vertebrates and invertebrates are so basic as to suggest an unbridgeable gap between them. Evolutionists still must satisfactorily explain how this remarkable transformation occurred.

5) **Furthermore, if evolution** took place, then species must gradually have changed into other species, over a span of millions upon millions of year. This change from one species to another did not happen overnight. There must have been many, many transitional stages between the species as we know them now. The cat was not always the cat we know now. There must have been many previous near-cat creatures that lived before the final result emerged.

But where are these links? Not only don't these intermediate forms exist now, but fossil remains of them have been lacking. What happened to the "missing links"? Even after a century of extensive archaeology, they are still to be found. Hundreds of isolated colonies of human beings were discovered under every imaginable environmental condition, and yet no trace of transitional forms exists anywhere. *Why not?*

(Some point to the eohippus, a small horse-like specimen, as an example of a missing link. However, even this evidence is not conclusive. It has been found that such cases of midget horses may be caused by poor feed, and that, when given proper nourishment, the horses grew to normal size. The eohippus, then, might have been in reality an undernourished specimen of the horse we have today.)

6) **Evolution is by definition** a gradual process, as we mentioned above. That means that only small changes occurred, possibly by means of mutations, over the years. In practical terms, then, the evolutionists would say that the evolving bird developed a wing slowly, bone by bone, inch by inch. That means that it took many generations until the wing was suitable for flight, since the

wing is an incredibly intricate limb. Yet that would mean that during all these transitional generations, the birds had to walk around with heavy and totally useless half-wings. A bird lugging around this non-functional limb should have had more difficulty running away from enemies than a bird without any developing wing. Yet, according to the evolutionists, the bird with half a wing was the more fit creature, and it was the one which survived best. This is totally contrary to logic!

Let us also consider the eggshell. The shell must be exactly the right thickness or the developing chick could not survive: If the shell is too thick, the chick cannot peck its way out; if it is too thin, the chick will not be protected against harm. According to the evolutionists, this proper egg thickness developed by trial and error. Until this happened, though, there must have been many problems. While the eggshell is evolving, how did the chicks inside survive? And if they could not survive, how were they able to create their own offspring? Birds should have died out with the first generation—yet they are certainly still with us today. How did they manage it without a G-d there to make sure the eggshell was perfect the first time?

There are many other similar examples. The cobra has an incredibly complex mechanism for producing and injecting poison into its enemies. How could this mechanism have evolved? Did the snake develop the ability to manufacture the poison before it had the ability to eject it? Then why wasn't it immediately poisoned itself? Or perhaps the snake developed the poison-injecting apparatus before it was able to make the poison. Yet why should this have happened? Did the snake's body somehow prophetically know that the snake would one day manufacture poison that would have to be ejected? Either way, a problem exists.

What about the eye? We have seen how complicated and adept it is. Unless all its parts are in place and are functioning properly, it is of little use. But, according to the evolutionists, it, too, could not have emerged full-blown overnight. It must have developed bit by bit, feature by feature. However, if that is so, it could not have been used for sight until all its components were in place. And why should organisms with an evolving, useless eye have outsurvived those creatures without it? The developing eye had no notion that it was going to become a source of sight. Nor did the developing heart, or lung, or kidney know that they were going to perform specific functions. They must have undergone long periods of change to turn into what they are today, according to the evolutionists. But during the time of development over the ages, they could not have worked very well. Then how could the transitional species with incomplete and non-functional organs have survived? And how could they have consequently paved the way for the intricate creatures that abound today?

There are additional such cases, but the point has been made. The evolution of various limbs and organs could have held little immediate benefit for the developing species. Rather, they should have been hindrances. Why, then, did the species with these developing parts have been more fit to survive than those without them?

7) **Since evolution took** place entirely by chance, it is against all odds to say that two different species evolving along different branches should have emerged with very similar features. That is like saying that men from two different cultures living in opposite isolated poles of the earth decide to write novels that turn out to be identical. This is not impossible, but highly unlikely. The different groups of species were supposed to have evolved along different pathways. Yet, consider the similarities between them. Birds, bats, and insects are all very different, yet all have wings. Fish and whales are not closely related —the latter is a mammal—but they both developed fins. Both vertebrates and anthropods have jointed legs and hinged jaws. Did lightning flashes-of-chance keep striking twice? Did these coincidences just happen to coincide? Or did G-d deliberately plan these similarities because they made the species functional?

8) **Evolutionist say that** vestigial organs show that man still has unneeded organs retained from earlier forms during the evolutionary process. Yet labeling certain organs as useless may come from pure ignorance. As time goes on, scientists are finding that organs once called unnecessary are indeed important. In the past, such parts of man as the thymus, the pituitary gland, the nicatating membrane, and the coccyx have been called vestigial organs. Later, scientists discovered that these helped in preventing infec-

tion, supplying physical support, and controlling growth. Even the once-derided appendix may have some effect in promoting the body's health. So these organs should not be written off as leftovers from earlier forms of life. They may be in the body because G-d put them there for a good purpose.

9) **The concept of** "Survival of the Fittest" is also not foolproof. If it were, then only the more complex organisms should really be considered worthy of survival. Yet, we find organisms like the opossum still with us and thriving, despite the fact that the opossum is a dull-witted, small-brained animal without any special survival talents. We find the one-celled animals and plants still with us, despite the fact that they are hardly complex. We also find man, with his ingrained potential for guilt feelings and embarrassment. Theoretically, those without shame should be more fit to survive than those with it, because they can act aggressively and have no remorse. But it is the very human man, with all his emotional frailties, who has survived. Could it be that G-d implanted these feelings within man to help him become a more humane creature? If not, why are these traits so prominent in man? (Besides which we must ask how such human features as emotions and a conscience evolved in the first place.)

10) **Evolutionists rely** heavily on fossils to substantiate their theory. Yet, fossil evidence is not always very neat. Many times, rock strata have shown the more complex fossils located below the less complex ones, indicating that the former existed before the latter and were buried first. Fossil pollen grains in the pine family have been found at the bottom of the Grand Canyon, despite the view of evolutionists that only much less complex plants lived when those rocks were formed. Man-made instruments have been found imbedded in coal even though evolutionists claim that coal was formed before man's appearance. Evolutionists say that tribolites were extinct long before man arrived on the scene; yet, a sandal-like print with fossils of tribolites was found in Utah. These findings do not fit the assumptions of evolutionary theory.

Evolutionary geologists have divided what they see as the earth's history into several time periods called eras. They have charted exactly what creatures appeared during which eras. Yet, nowhere in the world is there a rock formation containing fossils in the exact order of the charts. The Glacier National Park in Montana contains an overthrust in which Precambrian era rock rests on Cretaceous era rock beds, despite the fact that the latter is supposed to be 500 million years younger than the former. How did the reversal come about? Maybe the dating system is not entirely accurate. In fact, there is a vicious circle: Fossils are used to date rocks, and rocks are used to date fossils.

One might ask, "What about the seemingly conclusive evidence from the fossils of what evolutionists call "early man"? Don't the bones of Neanderthal and CroMagnon man indeed show that man evolved over the ages?"

Here too, these discoveries should not make us jump to quick conclusions. In most cases, very few remains were found--perhaps only a tooth or some jaw fragments. Nevertheless, from these few clues, scientists have taken it upon themselves to reconstruct an entire man, from head to toe. But who says that their imaginative reconstruction is entirely accurate? Perhaps they were guided by their theories of what man *should* look like rather than by trying to determine what man actually *did* look like. When the first fossil remains of mammoths were found, scientists projected ideas of how these creatures looked—only to change their ideas significantly when entire mammoths were found preserved in ice. The same may be true of human fossils.

Who knows for sure that the fossils are remains of typical examples of the period? When archaeologists find a skull and use it to reconstruct a sub-human man from it, how do we know that all other members of the species looked like that? Neaderthal man was at first depicted as being stooped and ape-like. It was then found that the specimen on which this assumption was based happened to be a lame, arthritic individual. He may have been an aberration. Furthermore, the fossils themselves might have been changed over the years by the pressure of cataclysmic events, such as the *Mabul* (Flood of Noach), a generally accepted fact, as we will see later.

In fact, scientists have been wrong about fossils in the past. At one time, they proclaimed that a certain Piltdown Man was a great fossil discovery—a link between man and ape that lived hundreds of thousands of years ago. After this evidence was accepted as valid by the greatest of scientists for fifty years, it was disclosed in 1953 that the Piltdown Man was a hoax, and that the fossil was really a man-made concoction of a modern man's skull and an ape's jawbone. Scientists are not beyond error in these matters.

All of the above arguments show that the Theory of Evolution is far from being unchallengeable.

Now consider what the Torah says regarding the creation of living things. It, too, states that the creation took place in stages, with the less complex organisms being created first and with plants preceding animals. It differs from evolutionary theory, though, in stating that the creation was carried out by a Divine Creator and that entire species were created in the same form that they have today. This would explain how the first cells and the first matter originated. It would answer the question of why no "missing links" have been found—*there weren't any.* It would also solve the problem of how organisms gained their complex body systems, and how so many different species came to resemble each other in various ways: *G-d created them like that,* so they could function properly on earth. Evolution presents contradictions and unscientific hypothesis. On the other hand, the Torah version of the creation of life raises no intellectual problems other than the "problem" of believing that G-d is capable of creation from nothing.

Question Six: Scientists claim that the earth is millions or billions of years old. Do they have proof that would contradict the Torah tradition that the earth was created some 5740 years ago?

Answer: Once again, we must stress that scientists can only guess when they predict the age of the earth. They were not personally present when the earth became a reality, nor was any other living creature. The earth has no birth certificate, no indisputable proof of its age. So no scientist can emphatically say that he is sure of just how old the earth is. In fact, scientists keep changing their estimates of the earth's antiquity. Just recently, some highly respected scientists said that the age most commonly assumed as correct should be cut in half. That means that they feel that earlier scientists overestimated by *several billion years*. Scientists are obviously far from certain about the matter.

The claim that the world is millions or billions of years old is based on secondary "evidence." It relies on the dating of the earth's rock and fossil samples, especially radioactive materials. For instance, scientists say that by comparing the relative amounts of uranium 238 and lead 206 in a rock, they can tell when the rock was formed. Similarly, they say that radioactive Carbon 14 in substances has been decaying at a fixed steady rate. By examining how much Carbon 14 a substance has left, scientists estimate its age. (However, Carbon 14 testing can help date only relatively new organic matter, so it is of limited use.)

Certain assumptions must be made for this method of dating to prove correct. The rate of decay of the original element (the Carbon 14, for instance) must have remained constant ever since the rock was formed and the substance could not have gained or lost any radioactive carbon isotopes in any other way. These assumptions should not be taken for granted.

For one thing, the earth might have been created in an already mature form. The Torah indicates that *Odom Ho'rishon* the first man, was placed on earth fully grown. It therefore follows that the earth itself might have been formed as a fully developed entity. That means that it could have begun as an already aged earth, and that its rocks contained already decayed original elements. Consequently, scientists might be adding many years to the earth's age in error. In addition, there may have been less carbon 14 in the atmosphere thousands of years ago, so that old fossils may therefore contain less of it.

Also, scientists might be wrong in assuming that the original elements have been decaying at a steady rate. Perhaps some cataclysmic events—changes in the earth's basic nature that cannot be reproduced in a scientist's laboratory—altered the rate of deterioration. Therefore, what some assume took thousands or millions of years to decay might have taken only hundreds of years, or even less. No one can say for sure. In fact, some scientists have noted that Carbon 14 testing sometimes greatly overestimates the age of objects.

Then there are other methods of dating the earth—such as by measuring the amount of meteoric dust in the solar system or the amount of helium in the atmosphere—that indicate that the earth's age can be measured in the thousands of years rather than millions or billions.

What is the Torah-based view of the earth's age? By calculating the dates of events listed in the Torah, scholars have concluded that our earth, as of the first of *Tishrei*, in the calendar year of 1979, was created 5740 and six days earlier. (There is another view that the creation occured in *Nisson* rather than *Tishrei*, but this does not change the basic figure.) The six days are important, for they represent the six days of creation mentioned in the Torah. A few authorities hold that the six days of creation may have had a longer duration than six ordinary days of our own experience, since our sun, which determines time, was not fully operational until later. (See *Rashi* on *Bereishis* 1:14 entitled *"Lehavdil"*.) This could extend the time period for the creation process. But even if one rejects this view, he must agree that these were not six ordinary days, but days of Creation, when the natural laws of the present were not yet in effect, and everything was being formed by the word of G-d. The processes of nature, and dating, may have worked faster during this time. Remember also that since the world was created mature and aged, ancient fossils (already appearing old) might have been created along with it. Finally, it is interesting to note that the *Midrash* mentions the possibility of worlds prior to the present one; some of the fossils and rocks found now may have come from them.

These factors show that the scientific findings, if actually correct (though this can't be proved), need not contradict the Torah chronology. At this point in time, it is doubtful whether any incontrovertible proof of the earth's age based on scientific discoveries will be found. What remains are scientific theories—which are disputable—and the dating of the Torah, which requires belief. We have shown that one can still believe in the Torah version without denying all the evidence proposed by scientists.

Question Seven: If all this is so, why do so many people nowadays accept the evolutionary theory and reject the idea of a Divine Creation?

Answer: The "Modern Age" is the age of Science.

According to a popular view of history, the period after the decline of the Roman Empire constituted the "Dark Ages". The one source of scholarship in the Western world at this time was the Church, but it abused its powers. It kept the world shackled in backwards Biblical beliefs, insisting on strict faith in G-d and puritanical behavior, and preventing all scientific investigation. Man was downplayed, and downtrodden. It took science to "free" him. This is the thrust of most modern-day thinking.

The scientific revolution was seen as a means of obtaining the truth through experimentation rather than mere faith. It allowed man to make himself, rather than G-d, the center of his sphere, and to investigate everything about himself and his world. He could explain awesome phenomena as being part of nature rather than G-d's work. This way, he had less need for belief in G-d, and less reason to live by the Church's strict moral code. He could relax his self-discipline, and indulge his human desires.

There remained only one problem: how to explain the world's creation. If G-d did indeed create the world, the Church's claims would be correct. Along came the theory of evolution, and G-d and the Church were no longer necessary. Now man had an alternate view of the creation of life that did not rely on the deeds of G-d. He was totally free at last.

This was the general feeling, especially among those wanting to seem sophisticated. They could claim to have progressed over outdated theological thinking. What made evolutionary theory especially attractive was that it had the seal of science. It was an idea based on scientific research, and science had the aura of truthfulness and respectability. If scientists said that life developed through evolution, they must be right.

Therefore, many accepted evolution with only a minimal amount of thought about the matter. For one thing, it seemed like a modern, "progressive" idea—an "advance" over the "stale thought of religion". For another, it allowed man to free himself from having to believe in G-d, and therefore, in having to obey His restrictions.

Finally, it was a scientifically-based idea, and scientists could do no wrong.

Certainly, the Torah agrees that the field of science is of major importance. For one thing, it allows man to study the wondrous ways of the world, and to gain a greater appreciation of G-d's handiwork. It can also enable man to utilize the earth's G-d-given resources to help his fellow man. So all men must be thankful to scientists for finding cures for diseases, developing new products for consumers, improving mankind's food supply, and uplifting man's material standard of living. To a Jew, these achievements are laudable because, among other things, they allow him to better serve G-d. Consequently, Orthodox Jews have been among the foremost scientists and doctors of the day; the Rambam and the Ramban, for instance were noted physicians. Science can indeed be a potent force for good.

At the same time, scientists aren't always the supermen that some consider them to be. They can be fallible. They have constantly challenged each other's views, changing their opinions to fit new evidence. For instance, for a while most scientists thought the atmosphere was filled with ether. We have also mentioned the matter of the Piltdown Man hoax. Einstein's Theory of Relativity challenged many previously sacrosanct beliefs about space. Even basic concepts about the atom have changed over the years. Scientists may be clever and gifted, but they are not always absolutely right. It should be remembered that beyond the simplest experimental stage, science involves philosophical premises that are subjective.

Therefore, just because many scientists endorse the theory of evolution, it does not mean that their word must be so. They have been wrong in the past, and they can just as easily be wrong again about the creation of life. Their attempt to remove G-d from man's purview has not made man intrinsically better. Crime, corruption, immorality and mass destruction are still with us. The Theory of Evolution has hardly freed man from societal problems. It has not led to moral progress.

Judaism disagrees with the view that religion stifles man's creativity or ability to examine the world. It does not feel that belief in G-d is antiquated or unsophisticated. One who is sophisticated enough to study the world's marvels can naturally come to believe in G-d. And one who believes in G-d can strengthen his self-control and treat others more charitably. Can anyone deny that this self-development represents true progress?

The Theory of Evolution must be examined carefully on its own merits. The fact that it seems "progressive" or "scientific" should not blind anyone to its inherent problems.

Question Eight: Even if we agree that G-d created the world, how do we know that He still regulates it? And if He does, why doesn't He make His presence more obvious, such as through miracles?

Answer: If one accepts the fact that G-d created the world with a definite purpose, it would make no sense to assume that G-d then cut off all contact with it. That would mean that the entire act of creation was nothing more than mere frivolity. If the affairs of the world after creation were of no interest to G-d, then what purpose would there have been in its creation to begin with?

The beginning of *Bereishis* stresses G-d's care in seeing to it that the world should be as perfect as possible: "And G-d saw that it was good." Would the all-mighty G-d have taken such pains to design the world if He were going to abandon it?

Furthermore the Torah makes it abundantly clear that He did not abandon it. The Torah describes numerous miraculous events—the splitting of the Red Sea, the ten plagues in Egypt, the giving of the Torah at Mt. Sinai—to affirm G-d's participation in worldly affairs. It tells of many encounters between selected men (Avrohom, Yitzchok, Yaakov, Moshe etc.) and G-d. It tells of how G-d's spirit was noticeably present in the holy *Mishkon* (Tabernacle) and later the *Beis Hamikdosh* (Holy Temple). G-d was certainly not "dead", or even "sleeping".

Some will ask why G-d does not seem to be taking so active a role in worldly affairs today. Why are there no bold and obvious miracles in our time, as there were in the days of Moshe Rabbeinu or Yehoshua? Why doesn't G-d make His presence more obvious?

We cannot, of course, read G-d's "mind", or state confidently why He does or does not do something. However, we can use our G-d—given logic to speculate that frequent clear-cut miracles nowadays would hinder G-d's world plan. One of the most basic tests of man's nature is his decision whether or not to believe in G-d. One who chooses to believe in G-d accepts with this G-d's commands of morality and charity; one who does not can reject them. The choice has a major effect on man's whole orientation, as we have seen.

Such a decision must therefore be an unforced one, made of man's free will. If man had no choice but to believe in G-d, then the act of choosing would lose its impact. Man would believe in G-d because he had to, not because he wanted to. He would be like a child who said he loved his parents because he knows he would be thrashed if he said anything else. Such a statement would have no meaning at all.

G-d, then, does not want to force man to believe in Him. He would not want man to behave like a robot or an instinctive animal, unable to make independent decisions. That was why He created man in His own image, with free will. That perhaps also helps explain why G-d does not reveal himself more obviously to the world today. If miracles were commonplace and the Divine presence were indisputably observable, man would have no choice but to say that G-d rules the world. It is true that miracles occurred long ago, but they were needed then to show a world that had no concept of G-d that G-d does indeed exist. They were necessary to make the Jews want to become a nation under G-d. Once that was established, there was no further need to belabor the point. Henceforth, G-d would make His presence felt in a subtle way, providing enough evidence of His existence to satisfy those who truly wanted to believe in Him.

What are these indications of G-d's presence? For some of them, we can turn to history. There was no indisputable proof of G-d's intervention during the story of Purim. Some could claim that the events that occurred then were the result of man's actions, not G-d's.

Nevertheless, the sequence of events—the killing of Vashti, the choosing of the Jewess, Esther as Queen, the foiling of Achashveirosh's assassination by Mordechai, the eventual downfall of Haman and the rise of Mordechai—eventually proved too orderly to have been a string of coincidences. The Jews prayed to G-d for help, and incredibly enough, they saw their enemy defeated and their leader take his place. There were no splittings of the seas or openings of the earth, for G-d worked within the context of natural events. Nevertheless, His guiding hand was seen by those who chose to see it.

Such hidden miracles—*nissim nistarim*—have occurred throughout history. We find Jews being saved unexpectedly from enemies (such as when Sancherev's attacking armies were suddenly plagued with illness and had to withdraw from Jerusalem). Conversely, we find Jews being punished when they did not deserve help (such as when internal jealousy led to the destruction of the second *Beis Hamikdosh*).

The very survival of the Jews to this day is perhaps the greatest miracle of all. By all odds, the small, persecuted and often homeless nation of the Jews should have faded from the scene centuries ago. Yet, they have not only survived, but they remain at the center of world attention. In our own times, events in the Middle East involving Israel have found a profound effect on the course of world events, and the problems of Jews in the Soviet Union have affected the course of East-West relations. There are Jews in numerous countries throughout the world today, still following the faith of their forefathers. If not for G-d's protection, how could the Jews have remained intact after all these years? The only answer is that G-d must be actively protecting them. And therefore G-d must be involved with our world.

If G-d's presence is felt on a national basis, it is also felt on an individual level. There are countless people who have labeled extraordinary experiences in their lives as "miraculous". All cases of survival against all odds, or any unexpected rewards, can be seen as acts of G-d. There are many such examples, which we call *hashgocho perotis,* or divine intervention in an individual's life. What, really is "good luck" if not *hashgocho perotis?*

Then there are the daily miracles of nature that we sometimes take for granted. Its marvels—the sunrise, the seasons, the life preserving cycle, the food chains, childbirth—are truly extraordinary. One who considers them carefully would conclude that they come from a Superior Being, and that without His continuous supervision, they wouldn't keep going. After all, even the most efficient of factories will stop functioning if left unsupervised for long.

So history, nature, and even our very own lives give hints that G-d is as involved with the world as ever. It is G-d's challenge to us to build a belief on these hints even when they are obvious.

Question Nine: If G-d controls the world, why doesn't life seem to run more perfectly? Why isn't there immediate reward for the righteous and immediate punishment for the wicked? Why do suffering and pain exist?

Answer: Questions like these have troubled many sincere, thoughtful individuals. They do not see how a G-d Who is righteous can permit catastrophes to harm man, especially if they strike those who seem to be good. How can events controlled by a G-d sometimes seem so unfair and unjust, they ask. How could horrors like the Crusades and the Holocaust have been allowed? They don't find ready answers to these, and they come to doubt the existence of G-d altogether.

In fact, there is no one pat, sure, easy answer to these questions (though there are, again, numerous possible responses, as we will soon see). This is because G-d works in ways that may not always be fully understandable to all generations of man. G-d has a master plan for mankind, which we are not privy to. So we may not find a logical reason for every occurrence, good or bad. But that does not mean that the reason does not exist. Man simply may not have the foresight or insight to see it.

This is especially important when considering matters of triumph and tragedy. We assume that when someone gets rich or gains a job, these are rewards; while if one becomes sick or poor, it is punishment. We then ask why these rewards do not go exclusively to those who do mitzvos, while the punishments do not go exclusively to those who do not. In man's view, this is what should happen.

G-d, however, may have a different perspective on the matter. What might seem a reward to man might, in the long run, not be so. The same is true of punishments. In fact, what might seem as a tragedy to one generation may strike the next as being, in hindsight, a triumph. For instance, Achashveirosh's decree against the Jews seemed a disaster to them at first, but it prompted them to pray to G-d for help, and this, in turn, led to their miraculous salvation. In retrospect, then, the disaster was in reality a blessing. So if a catastrophe appears to strike the Jewish nation at a time when it does not seem to deserve it, man shouldn't wonder. It may be part of G-d's far-sighted plan for mankind, and may turn out to be beneficial in the end. History is like assorted lines and dots which have no apparent meaning when seen at close range but which, when viewed from afar, form a complete logical picture.

The same is true of individual cases. Man may be wrong in judging what is a reward and what is a punishment—what is a good development and what is a harmful one. Money may seem the greatest reward for some. It can indeed help man live in great comfort. However, it can also prove a curse in the end. It can invite thieves and cause jealousy, and it can prompt man to indulge in sin. Similarly, fame might seem desirable, and it can boost one's ego. Yet, it can also lead to loss of privacy, great psychological pressure, and deep unhappiness. In recent times, Howard Hughes, Marilyn Monroe, Elvis Presley, and others reached pinnacles of prestige and accumulated great wealth—but died drained and depressed. Others who did not reach such popularity wound up with happier lives. So they were better off even if they didn't always think so.

In addition, some rewards and punishments are not visible to man on this world. Traditional Judaism believes that the world we know is but an introductory step to the world of the hereafter *(Olom Ha'Boh)*. After death, the righteous and the wicked are each given their respective just desserts. Therefore, it is possible that in this world the righteous sometimes receive punishment for their few sins, and the wicked enjoy brief benefits for their few good deeds, so that each will receive the full measure of their deserved fate in the World to Come.

As for pain, sickness, and suffering, they, too, may not always represent punishment. Consider the case of someone who can feel no pain at all. This might seem a blessing, but it isn't. Such a person will never learn what things are dangerous. He may think that it is perfectly all right to stick his hand into a fire, because he feels nothing; but, as a result, he will lose the hand. Pain is essential to the learning process, for it tells the body what to avoid. Sometimes suffering is also helpful—not only as a punishment for those who deserve it so that they will improve their behavior , but also as a way to make people appreciate life without it. Those who have been sick or injured took good health for granted until they lost it. Only then did they come to thank G-d for having something they previously considered commonplace.

Also remember that no one can ever be certain that he is indeed righteous and deserving of reward. This is only for G-d to decide, not man. Sometimes those who are seemingly good nevertheless harbor impure motivations or improper goals. Only G-d knows who deserves what. Perhaps those who are more naturally disposed to doing good, such as those who were raised with true love and care at home, must maintain an especially high level of righteousness, because more is expected of them. If they sin, their punishment may be more severe than those of others. Moshe Rabbeinu committed only one seemingly minor sin, hitting a rock for water instead of speaking to it. Yet, he was severely punished and was not allowed to reach his dream of entering the Holy Land, because he had higher standards to live up to, and he failed. No one can decide on his own just what treatment is due him. Only G-d can determine that.

Finally, it must again be stressed that man has free will. This has two implications for the topic we're discussing. For one thing, if punishment and reward were always immediate, man would lose this free will. He would be like an animal in a psychology laboratory, manipulated to act in specified ways due to rewards and punishments. If man were sure that he would always get a hundred dollars immediately after putting on *Tefillin*, the performance of the *Mitzvah* would lose its meaning. Man would put on *Tefillin* not becaue he really wanted to serve *Hashem*, but because he would be compelled to get the money. On the other hand, if someone would have a heart attack every time he did an *Aveirah* (sin), he would stop doing *Aveiros*—this because he was afraid of the heart attack, not out of fear of G-d. Man would become a conditioned animal, performing like a robot rather than a human with free choice. This would not be the man G-d created. Therefore, punishment and reward cannot always be automatic.

In a similar vein, man's free will means that he has the choice to bring happiness or suffering upon others. Wars and torture are not natural phenomena—they are instituted by man. Man can help improve conditions and decrease suffering in the world, but he must take the initiative to do so. Too often he has used his freedom of choice to cause harm.

It is clear that an all-powerful G-d is a G-d Who knows what He is doing. He does not, therefore, inflict pain on men or nations without cause. That man does not always see the cause is due to man's limitations. He cannot foresee the full flow of history. He cannot view what will happen in *Olom Ha'Boh*. He does not know who deserves what. He cannot tell whether an event will really turn out to be good or bad. These are within G-d's realm. Perhaps someday, G-d will reveal the mystery of His ways to man. Until then, it is up to man to have faith that everything G-d does is just—even if this may not be clear at the moment. He must remember that, when all is said and done, G-d remains perfect.

This is the definition of G-d.

SUMMARY OF PART ONE

In the first section of the book, we have discussed G-d and His ways.

We noted that because G-d is an unlimited, intangible, all-encompassing Deity, man—with his physical brain and limited understanding—cannot fully comprehend Him. Nevertheless, we have studied the manifestations of G-d in nature, and in the organization of the world and its creatures, which led us to the conclusion that G-d must indeed exist. No one else could have created a world out of nothing; no one else could have made the world function so effectively; and no one else could have brought into being as complex a creature as man. We considered the alternative of evolution, and found it wanting. It does not explain the origin of original matter, and cannot account for the incredible harmony of nature. The fact that all living things inherently strive to survive indicates that life has meaning—a meaning provided when G-d created the world.

Despite the evidence for G-d's existence, G-d Himself may not want to make His presence more obviously clear-cut. G-d wants to preserve man's sense of free will, to differentiate him from the animals. This may be why miracles no longer happen openly, and why reward and punishment are not always automatic. Nevertheless, for true believers, events and features of the world today give ample proof that G-d still regulates the world today and shows His personal concern for mankind. These believers serve G-d by free choice rather than out of habit or compunction, and this is what G-d wants.

These conclusions lead to new questions. What was G-d's purpose in creating the world? What might be the Divine Plan for mankind? Where does the Jewish nation fit into this plan?

This brings us to considerations of the Jews. They are called G-d's Chosen People. But who are they, and in what sense are they called "chosen"? What is their Torah, and what is their mission in life?

We will examine these questions in the next section.

PART TWO

THE REALM OF JUDAISM

PART TWO: THE REALM OF JUDAISM

Question Ten: What is a Jew, and what is Judaism?

Answer: A Jew is a member of a people unique in world history. No other group, nation, or religion have been quite like them.

On a legal level, one becomes a Jew in either of two ways:
1) Anyone born from a Jewish mother is automatically a Jew and legally remains one.
2) One who was not born from a Jewish mother can convert to Judaism.

It should be noted that conversion is not a simple one-step process. Rabbis make sure that the potential convert is sincere in wanting to become a full-fledged Jew before agreeing to convert him. They determine that he wants to convert for life, not out of a momentary infatuation. The potential convert is made to understand that many of the tasks required of an observant Jew are not easy. If he still wants to become a religious Jew, he is trained in the precepts of Judaism by Torah-observant Rabbis. The convert is also required to perform *tevilah* (immersion in a *mikvah*), and males must undergo *milah* (circumcision). This process contrasts with the aggressive missionary campaigns of some segments of other religions.

Mere legal definitions, however, cannot fully portray the totality of Judaism. To really become a part of the Jewish people, one must appreciate the Jewish heritage, study the Jewish traditions, and participate fully in the Jewish faith. Only one who whole-heartedly accepts his Jewishness and performs the prescribed laws can really know what it means to be Jewish.

What, then, is Judaism? Is it a nationality? Yes, there is a feeling of patriotism to the Jewish nation; an historic national homeland (Eretz Yisroel); and a national language (Hebrew). But Jews have existed as Jews in many different nations, even when Eretz Yisroel was not a sovereign state. They have also spoken other languages (especially Yiddish and Ladino) and been a part of foreign cultures while still retaining their Jewish identities. Therefore, one cannot limit Judaism to the definition of a "nationality".

Is it a religion? Of course, for Jews worship a G-d and perform religious acts. But the term "religion" also limits Judaism, and doesn't fully acknowledge its cultural and social influences on the world.

Others may say that Judaism is an ethical movement, for it helps guide man's behavior; or that it is a culture, for it has contributed much to the fields of art, music, and literature; or that it is a philosophy, for it has given man a framework in which to view the world. Still others identify Jews as an ethnic group, for they have certain unique traits and interact cohesively.

The definitions abound, but in the end, the question remains: What is Judaism and what are Jews? Actually, all of the above are true, and more, for here the whole is greater than the sum of its parts.

As those who are totally committed Jews know, being Jewish means having a firm identity as a person, a lifetime membership in a special group, a unique sense of spirituality, and a clear concept of the purpose of life. In essence, what makes Jews really unique is that they are the Chosen People.

Question Eleven: What is meant by the Jews being the "Chosen People"? What is the special "mission" of the Jewish people?

Answer: The Torah makes it clear that man was created for a specific purpose: to emulate G-d's righteousness on earth. At first, all of mankind was chosen for this task. However, early man failed in this mission, and allowed corruption and violence to predominate over justice and kindness. Therefore, G-d caused the Great Flood (*Mabul*) to eradicate the wicked. Thereafter punishment for failure was to be on a national, rather than a universal level. Therefore, G-d then chose one specific nation to especially pursue this mission. The Chosen People would act as G-d's model nation on earth, demonstrating to the rest of mankind how to behave properly. This nation was the Jews.

The foundation for the Jewish people was laid by three *Avos* (forefathers), the first of whom (Avrohom) agreed to a pact with G-d called the *Bris Bein Habesorim*. This was a guarantee that Avrohom's descendants would receive Divine favor, provided they accepted G-d's leadership. The people further developed this heritage, under the leadership of Avrohom's son, Yitzchok, and Yitzchok's son, Yaakov (also called Yisroel, the basis for the term "Israel"). The nationality of the Jews was forged during the years of bondage in Egypt; there the people gained the insight that they were indeed different. Then came the confirmation of the bond between G-d and the Jews: the acceptance of the Torah at Mt. Sinai, when the Jews affirmed their commitment to their special status.

By becoming G-d's Chosen People, the Jews accepted certain responsibilities.

On an individual level, they would have to:
a) accept and worship Hashem as the One and only All-Powerful G-d; and
b) observe the 613 *Mitzvos* (Precepts) of the Torah, as well as the extensions of these laws devised by the Sages.

On a national level, all Jews were to create a community of G-d as a model of righteousness for other nations to copy. This would mean much more than just a collection of good individuals. It would establish a whole culture devoted to G-d.

These commitments, of course, meant that the Jews had to meet certain obligations not required of others. They were told to abstain from various acts (such as working on the Sabbath) that were permitted for other peoples. Jews were expected to maintain a higher level of moral purity. Their self-control and their devotion to a spiritual ideal would be more severely tested than other men's. They would be like royal princes, whose behavior would reflect on the King, and who, therefore, would have to act with greater care. Jews who did not live up to the standards set by the Torah and who behaved irresponsibly in public, would be causing a *Chilul Hashem*—a lessening of G-d's esteem in the eyes of mankind. Jews would be held accountable for such unfortunate acts. One Jew should, therefore, try to stop other Jews from desecrating G-d's law.

In return for their allegiance to G-d, the Jews would become an extraordinary nation. They would play a unique role in the history of the world, and would gain a homeland brimming with Divine favor. They would, in short, receive G-d's extra personal care and guidance. This would come about because they were a Torah nation, a model for other nations to follow.

The special requirements of Judaism have caused some to say, "It is hard to be a Jew." At times, this may be so. But anyone who accomplishes something worthwhile must make certain sacrifices. The finest musicians and athletes require long training and rigorous discipline to achieve their goals. The Jews, likewise, need the discipline of the Torah laws to help them realize their human accomplishments on this world. If the Jews had chosen the complacency of conforming to the world norm, they would long ago have faded into obscurity.

Question Twelve: Have the Jews benefitted from being G-d's Chosen People?

Answer: The Torah promised rewards to the Jews for being loyal to G-d. They would become as plentiful as the sands of the sea, and their land would blossom with produce.

These rewards were conditional ones, though. G-d would keep His promises *provided the Jews observed His Torah.* The latter was not always the case. The Jews did not always fulfill their obligations. They often turned to other gods, and were lax in keeping the laws, even during Biblical times. As a result, the Jews brought upon themselves G-d's wrath rather than His favor. The resulting punishment was more severe for them than for other nations, because more is expected of the Jews. When they fail to live up to the higher standards set for them, G-d's disappointment is all the greater.

Nevertheless, there is evidence that G-d has indeed favored the Jews with benign treatment over the years, in the following ways:

a) **The very fact of the Jews' survival to this day** is the best proof. The Jews are minuscule in number compared to other nations. Yet, no other people have existed for so long despite such adverse conditions as oppression, persecution and lack of a homeland for many centuries. Mighty empires have become mere memories, but the Jews are a living entity, still in the world's limelight. Jews are a tenacious people, but tenacity alone could not account for their survival. Divine help was also required.

The longevity of the Jewish people has led to the fulfillment of G-d's promise that the Jews would be fruitful and productive. This might seem far-fetched, in light of the Jews' relatively small numbers. True, they may make up only a very minor percent of the world's total population today, yet, if we take a retrospective view, and try to number all the Jews who have existed from time immemorial, we would have great difficulty. There have been so many generations of Jews, living in so many different countries and climes, that we would soon come to the clear conclusion that there have indeed been countless Jews throughout the ages. And their productivity has been such that there is virtually no society that has not benefitted from their presence. It was nearly 4,000 years ago that G-d guaranteed Avrohom that his descendants would be as numerous as the stars in the heavens. Since then, no nation has glittered so steadily on the world scene, as the Jews have.

b) **Direct Divine intervention** assisted the Jews in their time of need during Biblical days. Without G-d's help, they would never have left Egypt or survived the ensuing Egyptians' pursuit. Without G-d's help, they would not have emerged intact after forty years in the blistering desert. And without G-d's help, they would not have been favored with the holy land of Eretz Yisroel. Israel's emergence as a nation was literally a miraculous event.

Even when G-d's intervention on behalf of the Jews was not overt, His helping Hand was still noticeable. The delivery of the Jews from Haman's planned extermination in the days of Esther, the triumphs of the Chashmonoim at the time of *Chanukah*, the victories of the Israelis over the surrounding Arab armies can all be explained away by some as natural phenomena. For believers, though, they are signs that G-d has not abandoned His people.

c) **Jewish prominence in the world** has been remarkable, considering the Jews' small numbers. Almost all societies have encountered and often benefitted from the Jews, often without appreciating them. Jews labored for the Egyptian empire, which suffered greatly for abusing them. The Jewish state formed part of the Greek and Roman Empires, but its citizens revolted when oppressed. Judaism was the basis for the Christian and Islamic religions, but the Jews were ill-treated by the Crusaders and banished from many parts of Europe for their religious beliefs. The leaders of a 12th century Russian empire, the Khazars, converted to Judaism, but Jews were a special target of Russian Czars. Jews helped Spain become a wealthy world power, but their expulsion robbed the country of some of its finest minds and talents. Jews were with Columbus on his first voyage to America, and they became a major ethnic group in the United States. They were given special notice by leaders—from Alexander the Great and Julius Caesar to Napoleon Bonaparte and Adolf Hitler, who centered World War II around their attempted destruction. Restrictions on their emigration from the Soviet Union caused a chill in American—Soviet relations. Their wars with the Arabs resulted in an energy and economic crisis felt the world over. Jews have certainly remained newsmakers throughout their existence. Other nations have shone more brightly on the world scene at times, but they have quickly burned themselves out. The Greek and Roman Empires have long since disintegrated; Spain is now a minor power; the much-heralded German Reich collapsed after twelve years. Yet, the supposedly lowly Jews continue their noble trek through history, still vigorous and intact.

The contributions of the Jews to the world at large over the years have been extraordinary. It was the Jews who introduced the idea of monotheism—the belief in one G-d—to the world. The Jewish Bible has been studied by peoples throughout history as a guide to morality. The Jewish lifestyle has been admired as an example to be copied. Its emphasis on a closely-knit family, assistance for one's fellow man, and striving for scholarship has been highly praised. Jewish accomplishments in academic endeavors, the sciences, and the arts have been remarkable, especially in light of the proportionately small size of the Jewish people. Jews have been in the forefront of drives for greater humaneness and civil rights; their willingness to give charity is unparalleled.

Some have spoken of a special "Jewish mystique" to explain the unusually high level of Jewish achievements in the world. Mark Twain wrote the following about Jews in 1899:

> "If the statistics are right, the Jews constitute but one per cent of the human race. It suggests a nebulous dim puff of star dust lost in the blaze of the Milky Way. Properly, the Jew ought hardly to be heard of; but he is heard of, has always been heard of. He is as prominent on the planet as any other people, and his commercial importance is extravagantly out of proportion to the smallness of his bulk.
>
> "His contributions to the world's list of great names in literature, science, art, music, finance, medicine, and obtruse learning are also very out of proportion to the weakness of his numbers. He has made a marvelous fight in this world in all ages; and has done it with his hands tied behind him. He could be vain of himself and be excused for it. The Egyptians, the Babylonians, and the Persians rose, filled the planet with sound and splendor; then faded to dream-stuff and passed away; the Greeks and Romans followed, and made a vast noise, and they are gone; other people have sprung up and held their torch high for a time but it burned out, and they sit in twilight now, or have vanished.
>
> "The Jew saw them all, beat them all, and is now what he always was, exhibiting no decadence, no infirmities of age, no weakening of his parts, no slowing of his energies, no dulling of his alert and aggressive mind. All things are mortal but the Jew; all other forces pass but he remains. What is the secret of his immortality?"

In fact, there is no secret at all. If the Jews have been uniquely productive, it is because G-d made them so, to befit a Chosen People.

d) **The personal happiness of the Jews** is another factor to consider. In view of all the oppression and poverty Jews have known, one might not expect them to be happy with their lot. Certainly, many Jews throughout history have been deprived of the riches and luxuries usually associated with happiness. It may seem odd, then, that it was particularly those Jews who lived under deprived conditions who almost never converted to another religion. Given the choice, a large number actually selected death over conversion. Why? Because Judaism can provide its adherents with a superior satisfaction: that of knowing one's identity and mission in life. A Jew feels the fulfillment of living a morally upright life as a member of a supportive, cohesive group. Above all, a Jew knows that his life is one of *Emes*—truth. He can be sure that, if he follows the Torah, his life is being lived correctly, because G-d has told him so. This brings a deeper sense of satisfaction than money can ever supply. Inflation can make money worthless, but a moral, worthwhile life can never lose its value.

Ironically, it is only recently, when Jews have been allowed to join the middle class, that many of them have assimilated and abandoned their faith. The diluted brand of Judaism experienced by so many non-religious Jews today emphasizes the material over the spiritual, the dollar over the Deity. These Jews seek solace in wealth and weakened values, and they often find their lives spiritually empty. Their marriages dissolve, and their children lack direction. They never know the happiness of the involved, committed Jew. This is one of the great tragedies of the Jewish people today.

e) **The Jewish place in the World to Come** is stressed by the Torah and its Sages. We preface the reading of *Pirkei Avos* (Ethics of our Fathers) on *Shabbos* during the summer with the statement that "All of Israel have a portion in *Olem Ha'Boh,* the World to Come. " Clearly, no one can disprove this. No one can dismiss the Jewish concept of the *Neshomoh,* the Divine soul. Jews believe that every person is endowed with a G-dly spark that elevates him above the level of an animal. It helps him strive for a spiritual reunion with his Creator, and it transcends the mortality of the body. Jews believe that the *Neshomoh* survives death, and, if the person's earthly acts have been good, enters the blissful sphere of *Gan Eden.* This is the reward for a life well lived, and Jews have a special opportunity to gain it.

The very fact of death, an inevitability that even atheists must face, should make non-believers think again. They must always wrest with the possibility that there is, after all, spiritual life after death. They must always cope with the thought that they will find a just dessert awaiting them after they die. This can prove very agonizing, especially at the end of one's life, when it is almost too late to undo a misspent existence.

We should make it clear that all of the above is not meant to imply that other nations and peoples do not share G-d's favor. On the contrary: G-d views all living things as His beloved creatures. Righteous members of all groups and religions are also promised eternal rewards. Nor does the above give Jews the right to be drunk with arrogance. The choseness of the Jews may have given them certain benefits—but they should remember that it carries with it extra responsibilities, too.

Question Thirteen: Why has there been so much anti-Semitism throughout history if G-d is supposed to protect the Jews?

Answer: It is true that anti-Semitism has been a persistent problem. It was present in Egypt when the Jews first became a people, and it is certainly evident in the "civilized" world of today. One only has to consider such recent events as the oppression of Soviet Jewry, the opposition to Israel in the United Nations, and, of course, the Holocaust of European Jewry perpetrated by the most "cultured" of nations, Germany, to see that anti-Semitism has hardly disappeared.

Why is this so? Why might G-d permit this? We cannot read G-d's "mind" to know for sure, but there are a number of possible explanations for His permitting hatred of the Jews.

1. **Sometimes G-d may use** other nations as a means of punishing the Jews for neglecting the Torah. For instance, it may not be coincidental that the terrible Russian pogroms in the 1880's came after many Jews attempted to assimilate into Russian society, and that the Holocaust began in Germany, where many Jews tried to be more German than Jewish. (However, it must be made abundantly clear that this does *not* imply that all victims of anti-Semitism were sinners.)

Morever, the Torah itself states that when the Jews forsake G-d, enemies will gain the upper hand over them. The *Tochacha* section (Devorim 28:15 ff) is quite explicit in describing the catastrophes that will befall the Jews if they turn from G-d.

2. **However, it should also** be noted that in many cases a catastrophe for Jews was followed directly by a beneficial develop-

ment. G-d may punish His people, but He also gives them a chance to correct their mistakes. The oppression in Egypt led to the consolidation of the Jewish people. The destruction of the second *Beis Hamikdosh* was followed by the compilation of the *Talmud*, which enabled Jews to study the Torah wherever they were. The expulsion of the Jews from Spain was followed by Columbus—possibly a Marrano himself—setting sail from Spain to discover a land that would one day prove very hospitable to Jews. The pogroms in Russia led many Jews to leave for Israel and America, helping them to avoid the repression of Soviet Jews during the mid-1900's. The Holocaust was followed by a new network of Yeshivos in America and Eretz Yisroel and the resettlement of many Jews and Torah centers to these lands. G-d, then, always seems to offers His chastened people new opportunities to win His favor.

3. **At the same time,** anti-Semitism has ironically helped strengthen feelings of Jewish identity and brotherhood. Jews never seem to feel more Jewish than when they or their fellow Jews are under attack. They then usually put aside rivalries and materialistic goals, and unite against the common enemy. In a way, then, anti-Semitism has helped keep the Jews together as a people, and has constantly reminded them that they cannot simply blend into the world fabric. It is sad that it should take hatred to keep the Jewish nation intact, but this has been a fact of history. It is something that one must bear in mind when considering the total effect of anti-Semitism.

Question Fourteen: Can a Jew escape his Jewish identity?

Answer: Certainly, enough Jews throughout history have either challenged Jewish law, attempted to convert to other religions, or tried to assimilate into the non-Jewish society. Even while the Jews were in the desert, many murmured against G-d, and Korach led a rebellion against Moshe. Other breakaway sects have included the Karaites and the Maskilim, and, in a certain way, the Christians. Particularly during the past two centuries, Jews have tried to escape their identities by changing their names, their lifestyle, and their values. They have tried hard to make the world forget that they are Jews.

Why this attempt to escape the Jewish label? There are several possible reasons:

1) Many may have found the task of being observant Jews too difficult. They feel that they cannot remain observant and members of "modern society" at the same time–despite the fact that many Orthodox Jews have been able to do so.

2) Others may have missed the opportunity to grow up in a true Jewish environment, and may not have known the positive aspects of being observant. They, therefore, reject tradition out of ignorance, though they can still experience true Judaism later in life.

3) Others may have tried to escape anti-Semitic attacks by hiding their Jewishness—but this escape has not always proved successful, as we will soon see.

4) Some have converted to gain entry into a wider social circle, or to be able to intermarry.

5) Others may have experienced some personal tragedy that led to a loss of faith in G-d and His laws.

6) Yet others may have a need to rebel against what they consider the authority of a religion.

7) Finally, some may have forsaken G-d because they have found a new deity in money and materialism. They then considered Judaism an obstacle in their drive for economic mobility.

Nevertheless, Jewish law states clearly that a *Jew is a Jew and will always remain a Jew*, no matter how far he drifts from Judaism. He may no longer be a good or loyal Jew, but his basic identity remains. There are a number of reasons for this:

1) **Judaism believes that each Jew is born with a "Jewish Neshomoh"**—an innate bond to Judaism that may weaken but never disappears. Even when one denounces his Jewish heritage, his ties to his people can resurface. We have seen this happen time and time again, when the Jewish nation has been threatened (e.g., the sudden resurgence of Jewish consciousness during the Arab-Israeli wars); or during times of personal crisis; or when one is older and face-to-face with his mortality. It is often when one is down that he first appreciates the strength of spirituality, and the power of prayer. It is at these times that the Jewish spirit arises seemingly from nowhere—and thus we have the unexpected phenomenon of non-observant Jews returning to the fold.

2) **Societal insecurities often make people reexamine their "roots."** They want to be reassured that their heritage is intact, and that they come from a line of survivors. This is why geneological journeys to the past have been popular recently. Certainly Jews prove second to none in boasting an illustrious past. Jews can take pride in their ancestry. And even if members of one or two generations have strayed from their religion, their descendants might want to return to it. Therefore, Judaism does not recognize one's right to sever all ties to it. Why should someone be allowed to deprive his descendants of a heritage they might want to eagerly accept?

3) **Finally, every Jew must remember that, religious or not, he is still a Jew in the eyes of non-Jews.** No matter how assimilated a Jew might be, he will be identified as a Jew during times of crisis, when the chips are down and the lines are drawn. Many German Jews were sure that they had gained full-fledged membership in gentile society. They were stunned to discover that, in the clutch, they were shipped out to the concentration camps along with the other Jews. Not only that, but even those Jews who had converted to another religion were still labeled as Jews. For in the eyes of gentile society, a Jew is always a Jew, no matter how diligently he tries to hide it. Karl Marx, Benjamin Disraeli, and Heinrich Heine were among those who were still considered Jewish even after their own or their ancestors' conversion.

On the other hand, when religious Jews gain the limelight, they win respect for having remained steadfast in their convictions. They have not downgraded their origins just to gain favor in men's eyes.

Question Fifteen: What is the Torah?

Answer: The Torah is G-d's legacy to the Jews and to the world. The word "Torah" is derived from the term "*L'Horos*", meaning "to teach". The Torah is replete with G-d's teachings of morality and philosophy. It is the blueprint for a proper Jewish society.

The Torah was transmitted to the Jewish people at Mt. Sinai, an act that signified the birth of Israel as a nation with a purpose. The Torah is therefore, in a sense, the constitution of the Jewish people. But it is a constitution devised by G-d rather than by man.

Actually, the Torah consists of two complementary parts: the *Torah She'B'Ksav*(Written Torah) and the *Torah She'B'al Peh* (Oral Torah). The *Torah She'B'Ksav* consists of the five *Chumshei Torah: Bereishis, Shemos, Vayikroh, Bamidbor,* and *Devorim.* These show the development of the Jewish nation, from the creation of the world through the death of Moshe, as the Jews were about to enter the Holy Land. They also contain the codes and beliefs that are basic to Judaism. The events of the *Chumash* are followed up in the seforim known as the *Nevi'im* and *Kesuvim,* describing the Jews' history from the leadership of Yehoshua to the building of the second *Beis Hamikdosh.* Here, too, are philosophical concepts that form the foundation of Jewish theology. The three sections of the *Torah She'B'Ksav—Torah, Nevi'im, Kesuvim—* are together referred to as the *Tanach.*

The *Torah She'B'al Peh* is equally important, being a thorough explanation of the *Torah She'B'Ksav.* Its precepts were also imparted at Mt. Sinai. However, unlike the *Torah She'B'Ksav,* which was by definition always in written form, the *Torah She'B'al Peh* was originally transmitted orally, from one generation to another. This was done so that Jews would devote more time to examining the Torah carefully with others. It ensured their learning the law from an expert who could explain it in the proper way. It was only when the *Torah She'B'al Peh* was in danger of being forgotten, because of adverse societal conditions, that Rabbi Yehuda Hanosi began to arrange it in written form. His endeavors became the six orders of the *Mishna,* which was completed around 3948 (188 C.E.). Explanations of, and commentaries on the *Mishna* were compiled by succeeding Rabbonim, and are known as the *Gemarah.* There are two versions of the *Gemarah:* the*Talmud Bavli,* compiled by Rav Ashi in Babylonia, and the*Talmud Yerushalmi,* compiled by Rabbi Yochanan in Eretz Yisroel. The combined text of the *Mishnayos* and *Gemarah* is often termed the *Talmud.* Those who have delved into the study of *Talmud* know that it is an unparalleled composite of practical law, philosophical discussion, logical arguments, and moralistic stories. It is no wonder that the *Talmud* has intrigued scholars for centuries, and has remained the bread and butter of the Jewish people.

Literally, the word "*Gemarah*" means completeness, for its

composition marked the final depiction of G-d's words at Mt. Sinai. However, man's study of these words continues to the present day. Torah scholars have contributed a non-ending series of commentaries and teachings on the Torah, helping to impart the Torah's messages and laws to new generations. These *Rabbonim* have been grouped into the following categories: *Rabbonon Savoraim* (ca. 475-590 C.E.), *Gaonim* (590-1038 C.E.), *Rishonim* (11th to 15th centuries), and *Acharonim* (16th century and later). Among these *Rabbonim* have been such outstanding scholars as Rashi (whose commentaries on the *Tanach* and on the *Talmud* have elucidated them for all succeeding generations), the Rambam (whose philosophical and legal works have helped countless Jews appreciate the core of Judaism), and Rabbi Yosef Karo (whose supreme legal code, the *Shulchan Oruch,* clarified the exact duties of the Jewish people). Works on the Torah continue to be written year after year, evidence of the never-ending relevance of its teachings.

This, then, is the Torah: the sum total of G-d's message to the Jews and to mankind, replete with philosophic and moral aims woven into a practical, legalistic fabric.

Question Sixteen: Why do Jews consider the Torah so important? Why do they place so much emphasis on learning Torah?

Answer: The Jews do not think of the Torah as just a book of literature or law. It is not a simple primer in religion, or a series of fables about the origins of the Jews. It is not something whose essence can be captured in a short summary or a three-hour movie version.

Rather, Jews consider the Torah an all-inclusive "Blueprint for Life". It supplies a rationale for life's purpose. It offers practical advice on establishing a humane society. Nothing is beyond the purview of the Torah. A *Mishna* in *Pirkei Avos* (Ethics of the Fathers) summarizes the Torah's value: "Occupy yourself with It again and again, for everything is in It." The Torah is G-d's wisdom revealed to man. Without it, the Jews would have floundered as yet another lost nomadic tribe in the Middle East. With it, the Jews can act as G-d's people.

Consider the five books of the Torah. Some books have dismissed them as nothing but mythological Bible stories accompanied by outdated laws. What they don't realize is that the Torah has eternal messages for man, among them the following:

a) The laws basic to any successful human civilization, such as the *Aseres Hadibros*, (Decalogue, often called the "Ten Commandments"),

b) An absolute, objective clarification of right and wrong,

c) An intimation of the meaning and goals of life, and

d) A plea for righteousness and brotherhood throughout the world.

Our Sages have said that the Torah's purpose is to promote compassion, peace, and loving kindness for all times in all places.

For the Jews, the Torah has the additional function of explaining the origins of the Jewish nation; depicting role models for Jews in the persons of Avrohom, Yitzchok, Yaakov, Soroh, Rivka, Rochel, Leah, Moshe and other righteous individuals; outlining the 613 eternal *Mitzvos* (laws and precepts) on which the Jewish religion is based; and revealing how the Jews are to serve as G-d's emissaries in setting good examples for the rest of mankind. The Torah is the Jews' passport through history.

The other parts of the total Torah—the *Nevi'im, Kesuvim, Talmud,* Commentaries—have classified and further developed these basic teachings. They have provided correct interpretations for Bible passages that might be obscure. (The Torah itself does not explain every single idea in painstaking detail because this would make it much too complex for the average person to comprehend. In their brevity, the first five books of the Torah have become easily accessible to every person, not only the scholars.) They have provided inspirational stories—like those of *Esther* and *Ruth*, as *well as the Medrashim*—poetic insight into life's meaning—*Tehillim* (Psalms), *Mishlei* (Proverbs), *Kohelles* (Ecclesiastics), *Iyov* (Job)—historical background—*Yehoshua, Shoftim, Shmuel, Melo- chim*—indicators of the destiny of mankind—*Yeshaya, Daniel*—and practical advice on everyday life—*Avos,* and much of the *Talmud.*

It is no wonder that the Torah has been compared to an ocean. A Jew without Torah is as lost as a fish without water. It is *the* Book that elevated the Jews from the status of just another group of people into a nation that flourishes to this very day.

It is because the Torah provides so much basic insight into life that it is taught to Jewish children almost from birth. Jewish youngsters who receive a religious education grow to appreciate the Torah in stages, progressing from *Chumash* and *Nevi'im* to *Mishna* and *Gemarah*, all the while studying each in greater depth. But because the treasure chest of Torah is so vast and complex (the *Talmud Bavli* alone contains over 30 different major units, each quite lengthy) and because much of the Torah can be comprehended only by mature minds, the learning process continues throughout one's entire life. This is why it is said that no one can truly "finish" the study of Torah. There is just too much to know, too many new insights with every review, for one to claim that he has mastered all of its wisdom.

Furthermore, the very study of Torah is a *Mitzvah* in itself. For many, the study of Torah (often in partnership with others, so that views can be exchanged and ideas clarified) is so stimulating and satisfying that full time Torah learning is a *Mitzvah* very easy to fulfill. There are very few experiences that can compare to finally comprehending, after many hours of aggressive mental labor, one part of G-d's Torah more clearly.

Finally, it should be stressed that the study of Torah is never truly fulfilled unless the deeds one learns about are actually carried out. Torah study is not just an academic exercise. One should be so impressed by the righteousness of the forefathers and G-d's concern for the unfortunate that he becomes a more humane individual himself. One who is an expert in theoretical law but who behaves reprehensively in public has no claim to Torah knowledge. The true Torah scholar makes himself known through his exemplary ways. He should be the living example of his studies.

Question Seventeen: How do we know that the events described in the Torah really took place?

A*nswer:* How does one prove that history actually happened? How do we know, for instance, that someone like Julius Caesar really lived? After all, neither filmed accounts of his actions nor recordings of his voice exist. Certainly, no one now alive can claim to have seen him in person. Yet, historians agree that a Roman leader named Julius Caesar indeed lived many centuries ago.

How do they know this to be so? They rely on a number of sources: books that were written about him and his exploits; stories about him that originated during his lifetime and were passed on to later generations by word of mouth; documents, records, and art that date from his era; and historical developments that resulted from his actions, affecting the fates of many every day of his life. We do not doubt that he once lived. All those generations who accepted his existence as a fact could not have been wrong.

Now we come to the authenticity of events described in the Torah. Here again, no one alive can testify to having seen Avrohom or Moshe Rabbeinu, and no television cameras were there to film the splitting of the Red Sea. Nevertheless, this does not mean that the personalities and the occurrences of the Bible are myths, as some eagerly claim. With the passage of time, more and more evidence has been amassed backing up the data supplied by the Torah.

One cause for belief comes from simple logic. No one doubts that the Torah is very old. The discovery of the Dead Sea Scrolls in 1947 proved that. These Torah scrolls had lain undisturbed since the time of the second *Beis Hamikdosh*, a period of some 2,000 years—showing that the Torah we have now is the same Torah the Jews had then.

Those who lived at the time the Dead Sea Scrolls were written were not too far removed from the events described in *Tanach*. More time has elapsed from the days of Julius Caesar to our own time, than elapsed between the Exodus from Egypt to the destruction of the second *Beis Hamikdosh*. If the Jews of that time had any reason to doubt the existence of Moshe, the leadership of the Judges, or the existence of the Jewish Kings, they would certainly have labeled the *Tanach* a fraud. Would the early generations have passed down tales of the Torah—especially those with negative implications, like the sin of the Golden Calf or the losses to various Cannanite countries—if these had not occurred? Would they have based their religion on a fabricated history that could easily be disproved? Would the early Jews have accepted a Torah with so many difficult laws if they had not actually experienced the Divine Revelation at Mt. Sinai or seen the splitting of the Red Sea? That they *did* live according to the Torah and did *not* challenge its history are evidence of its veracity.

Perhaps even more compelling proof comes from the archaeological finds made during the past century, many of them confirming Torah statements. Archaeologists digging in the general area of the Middle East have discovered many old ruins, artifacts, and inscriptions which coincide with facts listed in *Tanach*. It should be remembered that digging continues, and that further finds may be forthcoming; that recent finds in Syria are being withheld from scholars for political reasons; and that the climate of Eretz Yisroel has not been very beneficial for the preservation of records and ruins. Consequently, there are many gaps in the archaelogical discoveries covering the Biblical area. What does exist, though is still very impressive, and some of the finds are described below:

1. **The Torah, in** its description of the Creation, states that smaller, less complex organisms were created before the more complex ones, and that water-based organisms and plants preceded the animals. This was written down long before any geologists existed. Yet, these statements have now been confirmed.

2. **There is plentiful** evidence that the Flood of Noach took place. For one thing, many different and far-flung nations—who did not have any way to communicate with each other—have handed down almost identical written accounts of a great flood, long ago. Among these nations are the Babylonians (whose "Epic of Gilgamesh", discovered around 1900, tells of a god called Ea telling a man named Utnapishtim to build a ship to escape the flood with his family and animals), the Chinese (in whose traditions a man named Yao builds the ship), the Indians (who called the ship builder

Satyavrata), and the Mexicans (who called him Coxcox). It is absurd to say that all these peoples made up the very same story out of cloth if it did not actually happen. This is especially true in view of the fact that all the accounts place the flood at about the same time period (some 4000 years ago), and that excavations have shown the local populations in the Middle East suddenly dropping drastically at this very time.

3. **The Torah tells** the story of the Tower of Babel, during which men tried and failed to build a tower to the heavens. Impossible? Hardly. Among the remains found at what was once called Babylonia (also known as Babel) have been ziggurats, immense towers that sometimes rose to hundreds of feet, just as the Torah account indicates. Another feature of the Tower of Babel story is that this marked the time when the people were dispersed and began speaking different languages. This indicates that prior to this there was only one universal language. It is therefore, interesting to note that many Greek and Roman (and therefore English, French, and German) words bear a striking similarity to their Hebrew counterparts. For instance, the Hebrew "*eretz*" is transplanted as "earth" or, in French, "terra"; "*sappir*" becomes "sapphire"; "*peri*" becomes "fruit" or "frucht"; "*yayin*" becomes "wine" or "vin"; "*ayin*" becomes "*eye*"; "*orev*" becomes "raven" or "corveau"; and "*shesh*" becomes "six" or "sechs". Similarly the English alphabet of today is derived from the Greek letters, which were in turn based on the Hebrew-Semitic alphabet. The very term "alphabet" shows the influence of Hebrew, whose first two letters are "aleph" and "bet". The letters themselves are almost identical: Aleph-alpha-A; Bet-beta-B; Daled-delta-D, etc. This is not necessarily conclusive proof that all languages stemmed from Hebrew, but it shows that we should not rule out the Torah indication that there was once a universal language.

4. **The Torah states** that Avrohom Ovinu was born in Ur Kasdim (Ur of the Chaldees). Many doubted that such a site ever existed. However, in the late 1920's, Sir Charles Woolley led an expedition that excavated the ruins of Ur near the Euphrates River in Mesopotamia. They indicated that Ur was quite a well-developed city heavily involved in idol worship, agreeing with the Torah account.

5. **The Torah describes** the cataclysmic destruction of the cities of Sodom and Amorah. Searchers have determined that the Dead Sea, which is in that area, is unusually deep—some 1200 feet below sea level. There is evidence that Siddim, where Sodom and Amorah were located, dropped abruptly, and was submerged under water, possibly the Dead Sea. The sea remains remarkably salty, and dead trees encrusted with thick layers of salt rise from the shallows—recalling the Torah statement that Lot's wife turned into a pillar of salt.

6. **The Torah says** that Avrohom's marriage to Hagar, Sarah's maid, produced a son, Yishmael, who became the father of the Arab peoples. Arabs today still revere Avrohom and Yishmael for that reason, and pray at the forefather's traditional burial place of the Machpelah in Hebron. Furthermore, the Arabs have had the custom of circumcising their sons at the age of thirteen—exactly the age at which the Torah says Yishmael was circumcised.

7. **The Torah says** that Yoseph, the son of Yaakov, was sold to slavery in Egypt, eventually becoming chief assistant to Pharaoh. Some say that during this period, and the period of the Jews' stay in Egypt, that country was under the sway of foreign people called the Hyksos. This could explain why few written records were kept during this time; if any were written, they may have been destroyed by the Egyptians, who wanted to blot out evidence of this humiliation. Yet, it is interesting to note that an ancient canal on the Nile near the town on Medinet-el-Fiiyum (80 miles south of Cairo) is still called Bahr Yusuf (Yoseph's Canal)—evidence of Yoseph's influence. Also, the Torah records that when Yoseph became viceroy of Egypt, he was invested with a ring, Pharaoh's seal, fine linen clothing, and a chain around the neck. Pictures and murals still extant in Egypt show that this was exactly the method of investiture at that time. And the Torah says that when Yaakov Ovinu died in Egypt, he was embalmed. The ancient historian Herodotus corroborates this as being the exact way in which Egyptians buried their dead. The Biblical account is accurate.

8. **The Torah continues** by stating that after Yoseph's death, the Egyptians enslaved the Jews and made them build bricks and erect the storage cities of Pissom and Ramses. A rock tomb west of the Egyptian city of Thebes contained on its wall a series of

paintings depicting the life of the vizier Rekhmire. One such painting showed him with a rod in his hand overseeing the bricklaying done by foreigners, who are drawn with beards and lighter skins—a sign that they were Semites. In addition, both Pissom and Ramses are mentioned in Egyptian records, and one inscription reads "PR hauled the stones for the great fortress of the city of Pi-Ramses-Meni-Amun". Pi-Ramses-Meni-Amun is the Egyptian name for Ramses, and PR in Egyptian hieroglyphics refers to the Semites. Finally, paintings and excavations have also uncovered the remains of the cities of Pissom and Ramses, and both contained ruins of graneries and storehouses—exactly as described by the Torah.

9. **The Cairo Museum** has a monument on which the inscription celebrates the victory of Pharaoh Merenptah over the Libyans. On this monument, the words "people of Israel" are found. Pharoah Merenptah came to the throne around 1230 B.C.E., about half a century after the Jews entered Eretz Yisroel under Yehoshua's leadership. This monument testifies to the fact that the Jews did exist as a well-known nation at that time. Other documents of the era mention foreigners called the Habiru, which may be related to the word "Hebrews".

10. **During the time** of the Judges (*Shoftim*), the Jews were harassed by the *Pelishtim*, according to the *Tanach*. Egyptian records confirm the existence of this nation, listing them as the Peleste. The *Tanach*, in Amos, says that the Pelishtim came from Caphtor, also known as Crete. Discovery of Pelishtim crockery has led to their being traced back to Crete.

11. **The ruins of a fortress** at Tell el Ful (Givah) have been traced back to the first Israelite King, Saul. His successor was King David, who greatly expanded the Kingdom's territory. Ruins of cities defeated by David have been found, as well as the pool of Givon, mentioned by the *Tanach* as the place where the soldiers of Saul's general, Avner, fought.

12. **King David's empire** was consolidated by his son, Shlomo (King Solomon). The *Tanach* in *Melochim* I, 9:15, mentions that Shlomo planned the building of Chazor, Megiddo, and Gezer. This implies that the blueprint for construction in all three cities should have been very similar. Excavations led by Yigal Yadin in Israel

determined that the city gates unearthed at Hazor and Gezer were indeed the very same type as those previously found in the ruins of Megiddo. In addition, archaeologists have found the foundry used by Shlomo to produce the copper needed to build ships at Etzion Gever, as mentioned in the *Tanach.*

13. **Additional excavations** have brought to light proof of the existence of many later Jewish Kings. Examples: The "Black Obelisk" found at Nineveh, now in the British Museum, shows Yehu, King of Israel, bowing before the Assyrian King Shalmaneser III. Excavations at Tell-el Mutesillim in the 1920's uncovered a seal with the Hebrew inscription "Shema, servant of Yerovom", referring to a King of Yisroel. The Moabite stone stated, "Omri, King of Israel, humbled Moab many years." The ruins of Kuyundshik yielded an inscription from Esarhaddon stating, "I gathered together the kings of Syria and the kings from across the sea, Ba'al the King of Tyre, Menashe the King of Judah..." This confirms the *Tanach's* story of Menashe being taken captive by the Assyrians. The so-called Taylor Prism corroborates the *Tanach's* contention that King Chizkiyah did not accept Sancherev's authority, and that Sancherev, therefore, attacked Judah. The prism does not mention Sancherev's eventual defeat, for it would not list government failures. However, this defeat, a miraculous occurrence described in the *Tanach,* was recorded by the ancient historian Herodotus; and the *Tanach's* statement that Sancherev was eventually killed by *both* his sons (and not just one of them, as Babylonian chronicles say) was confirmed by the Prism of Esarhaddon. In addition, the Siloan Pool, dug by King Chizkiyah at the time of Sancherev's siege, has been unearthed, and its dimensions coincide exactly with those mentioned in the *Tanach.* And historical findings have explained why the *Tanach* says that, after Yisroel was besieged by Shalmaneser, king of Assyria, "they" conquered it after three years. The use of the plural pronoun ("they" instead of "he") made sense when records were found stating that Shalmaneser died during the siege, and that his successor Sargon completed the task. To be accurate, the *Tanach* accredits the victory to both of them.

14. **Subsequent events have** even more substantial backing. The French archaeologist Marcel Dieulefoy, who excavated the

Persian palace in the ruins of Susa, declared that the descriptions of the palace given in the book of Esther must have been written by someone who knew the palace well, for they were amazingly accurate. (The ruins had been buried for over 2,000 years before being rediscovered, so the writer of the Book of Esther must have lived at the time of the actual historical events rather than centuries later.) Coins of the revolt of the Chashmonoim, the basis for the holiday of Chanukah, are still in existence. The rediscovered ruins of Masada, now available for public viewing, had many artifacts describing the struggle against the Romans, as well as a *Mikveh* (ritual bathhouse) built in exact accordance with Jewish law. This last fact shows that the martyrs of Masada were well acquainted with Torah law, which has been handed down to us unchanged. In addition, remains from the stronghold of Betar have furnished writings of Bar Koziba, the famed freedom fighter known more popularly as Bar Kochba—some written by him personally.

All of the above examples—and they constitute just part of the still-accumulating evidence—have been cited to illustrate a point: that the history contained in the *Tanach* is not the wild imagination of a mythologist, or a concoction by a committee written hundreds of years after the events described. Later writers could not have had the historical records to make their versions so accurate. The so-called "Bible Critics" have no basis for denying the Torah's authenticity. The Torah is *"Toras Emes"*.

Q*uestion Eighteen: How do we know that the Torah is G-d given rather than the work of man alone?*

A*nswer:* Traditional Judaism claims that the Torah was transmitted by G-d to Moshe on Mt. Sinai, that Moshe transcribed the Torah, and that he in turn transmitted it to the remainder of the Jewish people. This is the same Torah that was then handed down from generation to generation, to our very day.

No one denies that the written Torah exists, or that it is old. What the question comes down to, really, is how do we know that the Torah was not written entirely by Moshe or others of his era without any divine guidance? To this there are a number of replies.

a) **The Torah contains** many laws that are difficult for one to keep. There are even laws called *Chukim*, for which no rational explanations are supplied; examples include not wearing wool and linen together and not mixing milk and meat. The Jews at the time of the exodus from Egypt were not a tractable people. They did not accept authority lightly, and they often complained about Moshe's leadership. Under normal circumstances, would all 600,000 Jewish men alive then have accepted the difficult demands of the Torah? Is it likely that they would have compliantly obeyed every law if Moshe alone had drawn them up? Moshe was only one elderly man, and he could not have enforced his authority alone. It is much more likely that the Jews agreed to accept the Torah commands because these had Divine backing—a fact made clear by the Divine appearance at Mt. Sinai. The Jews would not have accepted the Torah from a mortal like Moshe, but they did accept it from G-d Himself.

b) **Furthermore, there are** parts of the Torah that no mortal could have written—parts which could have been disproved by later generations, but which have in fact been substantiated. One example, as mentioned earlier, involves the order of creation. Certainly no mortal at the time of Moshe could have said with certainty that the plants and water-based animals were the first living organisms to be created—yet this is just what today's geologists say. How could a mere man have had the audacity to state (as the Torah does in *Devorm* 14:7-8) that only three species—the *Gomol* (camel), *Arneves* (hare), and *Shoffon* (coney)—chew their cud and have partially split hooves? Wouldn't he be afraid that some species he was not aware of could also have these characteristics? Only an omniscient G-d could know this—and in fact; no one has yet discovered any other animals with these features. And how could someone hoping to write an eternally valid Torah confidently predict that if the Jews do not keep the *Mitzvos*, their sanctuary will be destroyed and they will be dispersed throughout the world? What if this prediction did not come true? The Torah would then lose its authenticity. In fact, only an all-knowing G-d could have made so accurate a prediction. The Jews did sin, the *Beis Hamikdosh* was destroyed, and Jews remain in exile throughout the world to this very day. Similarly, the correct predictions of the Prophets like Yeshaya, Yirmiyah, and Yechezkel—such as foretelling of the destruction of the *Beis Hamikdosh* and the return after 70 years of exile—could have been made only with Divine assistance. The fact that the Torah dared make these predictions indicates that only *Hashem* could have been the force behind it.

c) **Simple logic leads** to the conclusion that Moshe would not have written the Torah as it now reads and originated its laws. A human leader—especially in those ancient days—would have described himself and his ancestors as godlike individuals without any flaws whatsoever. Yet, we find that the Torah presents Moshe and his predecessors with their full set of blemishes. For example, Moshe descended from the tribe of Levi, yet Levi is depicted as having helped kill Shechem, an act which the Torah severely condemns (*Bereishis* 49:6). Moshe's own brother and sister are shown acting improperly on occasion—Aharon by helping build the Golden Calf, and Miriam by speaking ill of Moshe. Moshe himself is shown committing the error of hitting a rock to obtain water. He is punished by not being allowed to enter the Holy Land. Had Moshe written the Torah entirely by himself, he would most likely not have included these negative pictures of himself, his family, and his people.

In addition, he would probably not have promulgated many of the laws we find in the Torah. Why would he have originated *Chukim*—laws without any obvious reason—when these would have decreased his popularity among an already impatient people? Why would he have dwelled so long on laws of Eretz Yisroel—a land he would never enter? Why would he choose Yehoshua rather than his own sons to succeed him as leader? Why would he have denied his fellow Levites a permanent portion of the Holy Land?

These factors and countless others argue strongly that neither Moshe nor any other human wrote the Torah, but that *only G-d Himself could have conceived a Torah so perfect that it is still so relevant today.*

SUMMARY OF PART TWO

We have seen in this chapter how the Jews emerged as a unique nation, divinely chosen to adhere to the Torah. Along with the choseness, though, came extra responsibility: the Jews must be G-d's representatives on earth, behaving in so exemplary a manner that others will follow their example. The Torah—consisting of the Written and Oral Torahs—provides the blueprint for the behavior expected of the Jews. By adhering to the Torah, the Jews have attained great spiritual heights and personal satisfaction. The people as a whole have persevered throughout history, contributing much to civilization. But when the Jews did not remain true to G-d, and did not live up to His expectations, they suffered.

The Torah, we have found, is not a simple book of fables, but a Divinely-composed treasure chest of basic philosophy, law, and history. We have seen how the historical events described in the Torah have often been verified by archaeologists, and we have shown how it is illogical to believe that the Torah was written by man.

But what specifically are the laws of the Torah? What is their purpose? How do these laws enable a nation to establish a model civilization, and how do they help people live more humane lives?

We will examine these questions in the next section.

PART THREE

JEWISH LAWS

PART THREE: JEWISH LAWS

Question Nineteen: What is the source of Jewish law?

Answer: Man-made law comes slowly and tortuously, through compromise and pressure, from fallible legislators.

Jewish law by comparison, arrived in a blaze of fire and glory, presented by G-d Himself.

Kabbolas HaTorah—the giving of the Torah at Mt. Sinai—was perhaps the peak moment in human history. An event of Divine revelation, of awesome miracles, it marked G-d's unveiling—before three million men, women, and children—of His holy law.

"Na'aseh V'Nishmah," said the Jews before *Kabbolas HaTorah*: "We accept the obligation of keeping the laws; now let us hear them." True Jews in every generation since, have accepted the same commitment.

The laws that were given at Mt. Sinai are called *Halachos M'd'Oraisah*. These can be subdivided into a number of categories. One group of laws are those that constitute the *Torah She'B'ksav*. These are stated specifically in the *Chumash*, the Five Books of Moshe.

These laws, however, are sometimes presented only in principle. They are explained in detail in the *Torah She'b'al Peh*, the Oral Law, which was also transmitted at Mt. Sinai. This Oral Torah was passed down from generation to generation, as mentioned earlier, without being written down. In this way, other nations could not have access to it and thereby claim it as their own—as they had the Written Torah.

The laws of the Oral Torah are numerous and complex, and it was no simple task for the early Sages to remember them all. To facilitate recall of these laws, and to allow for their application in new situations, the Sages were provided with the following aids: a) *Sevoroh* (Reasoning). The Sages could rely on common sense guided by the Torah insight, to implement the basic rules of the Torah in new situations. For instance, the Torah tells us not to carry an object from a public to a private domain on Shabbos. The

Sages then concluded that it was likewise forbidden for one to carry an object from a private to a public domain on *Shabbos*. *Sevoroh* was one way of deriving laws which had their basis in the Written Torah.
b) *Drash* (Exposition). This means that the Written Torah contains indirect indications of many laws in its text, but the Sages had to derive these laws through a set method of interpretation.
c) There are 13 hermeneutic rules that were used to interpret the Torah text, and they are called the *Midos She'HaTorah Nidreshes Bohem*. (They can be found in many *Siddurim* before *Boruch She'Omar*.) These rules were explained to Moshe at Mt. Sinai. The early Sages (until the completion of the *Gemarah*) used them to substantiate laws not stated outright in the Written Torah, but hinted at through clues in the text.

Then there are the *Halochos L'Moshe MiSinai*. These are laws revealed to Moshe Rabbeinu at Mt. Sinai, but not contained in the Torah and not derivable through the 13 hermeneutic rules. Examples are laws giving specifications for the preparation of a *Sefer Torah*, *Tefillin*, and *Mezuzah*.

The Torah has, of course, remained the source of all Jewish laws to the present. It was passed down in its entirety from generation to generation, explained in detail by the scholars of the day. During the time that the Judges and the Kings presided over Israel, the transmission of the law remained stable. Students of the Torah discussed it in detail and the *Sanhedrin* (the "Supreme Court" of Talmudic times) based their decisions on it. The upheavals during the Roman subjugation, however, caused fears that the Oral Law would be forgotten. It was therefore written down, and comprises the *Talmud (Mishna* and *Gemarah*) that we have today.

There is also another source for Jewish law: that formulated by the Rabbis, and called *Halochos M'd'Rabbonon*. The Torah specifically gives Rabbis, widely respected for their scholarship and piety, permission to establish laws that will safeguard the Torah tradition. For instance, the *Anshei Knesses Hagedolah*, first under the leadership of Ezra (established when the Jews returned to Eretz Yisroel after the Babylonian captivity), proclaimed laws about making *Kiddush* and reading the Torah. The *Halochos M'd'*-

Rabbonon could not generally contradict or remove a Torah-based law.

The *Chumash* and the *Talmud* form the basis for all Jewish law to the present. But they are not merely law books. They also contain history, philosophy, and moral insights essential to Jewish spiritual well-being.

The *Talmud* sometimes contains differences of opinion among various Sages, arising from different versions of the tradition, or different methods of reasoning. There arose a need for clear-cut *Sifrei Halochoh*—law codes—that would contain final decisions arranged in a clear order for ready consultation.

Furthermore, Jews began spreading throughout the world—settling in Europe, Asia, and America—and started encountering situations and conditions not directly covered by the Torah or the *Talmud*. They presented these new questions and cases to the Torah scholars of the day for answers. Thus, after the age of the *Amoraim*, who arranged the *Talmud*, the *Savoraim* and *Gaonim* compiled records of their decisions, called *She'elos U'Teshuvos*. These collections or responsae applied Torah principles to new cases. Later Rabbinical decisions were often based on these precedents. In addition, the new, varied conditions that Jews found themselves in led to different customs (*Minhagim*) as to how Jewish laws should be carried out. (For instance, although the basic marriage ceremony remains the same for traditional Jews everywhere, the exact details involved vary from culture to culture.) Specific law codes were, therefore, needed to clarify proper practice.

There have been countless *Sifrei Halochoh*, throughout history, but only a few can be mentioned here. They range in time from the days of the *Rishonim*, who lived in Europe a thousand years ago, to the very present.

Rabbeinu Yitzchak Alfasi, commonly called the Rif (1013-1103) was born in Algeria and later fled to Spain; he recorded the definitive halachic decisions of the *Gemarah*, omitting material that wasn't pertinent. The Rambam was so impressed with this work that he said that it could be disputed in only a very few cases.

The Rambam himself, (Rabbi Moshe ben Maimon, 1135-1204)

was the supreme Torah leader of his day and also gained fame as a philosopher and a physician. His *Mishna Torah* (also called the *Yad HaChazakah*) is a 14 volume law code arranged in a very systematic form, covering all aspects of Jewish life.

Rabbeinu Yaakov Baal HaTurim, the son of the Rosh, wrote the *Arba Turim*, comprising four sections: *Orech Chaim* (dealing with daily laws like *Tefillah*), *Yoreh De'ah* (laws of *Kashrus*), *Even Ho'ezer* (laws of marriage and divorce) and *Choshen Mishpot* (civil laws).

This was the basis for the *Shulchan Oruch* of Rabbi Yosef Caro (1488-1575), a digest of laws that proved immensely popular. Ashkenazic customs were added by the *Rama*, Rabbi Moshe Isserlis of Cracow (1530-1572). The *Shulchan Oruch* with the *Rama* became the universally accepted law code of traditional Judaism. An abridged version of the *Shulchan Oruch*, the *Kitzur Shulchan Oruch*, by Rabbi Shlomo Ganzfried, (1804-1886) has gained great popularity among the Jewish masses; and an in-depth commentary based on the *Orech Chaim*, the *Mishna Brurah* by the Chofetz Chaim (Rabbi Yisroel Meir Hacohen, 1838-1933) is also widely learned.

In our own day, the *Iggros Moshe*, by Rabbi Moshe Feinstein, *shlita*, is one example of the ongoing series of *halachic* responsae applying the timeless laws of the Torah to modern-day conditions.

Every Jew should be familiar with the basic Jewish laws, and he should be ready to consult a competent Rabbi if he has a question of how to act in a specific case. In this way, he can be sure that he is acting in accordance with the same Torah that the Jews received from G-d at Mt. Sinai.

Question Twenty: Why are Jewish laws necessary? What is their purpose?

Answer: Once again, we can categorize the laws of Judaism, in accordance with their different purposes.

1) ***Mishpotim***. These are laws that regulate man's relations with his fellow man. They include restrictions against murder, robbery, rape and adultery.

Every civilized nation has found it necessary to issue laws like these. Without them, anarchy would result. Man would feel no compunction over stealing from and even murdering others. Life would become a hellish horror. This situation has arisen in our own day. In societies where the law has been broken down, a reign of instability and terror has prevailed. The fact is that man has a great potential for evil, made worse by his need for self-gratification. If this potential is not checked, man can easily abuse the rights of others. Laws are therefore needed to remind man that everyone will benefit if the rights of all are protected. It should be remembered that *Mishpotim* did not come from human legislators,but rather from G-d. They are not there to protect political governments but to benefit G-d's creations. It should, therefore, be noted that *Mishpotim* are not only of a restrictive nature. Many are also positive directives, encouraging man to live in peace with others.

These positive laws (*Mitzvos Assei*) include honoring one's parents, visiting the sick and needy, giving charity to the poor, and assisting those who need help. The Torah's basic theme is "*V'ahavta L'reiacha Komochah:* **Love Your Fellow Man As Yourself**". This, of course, leads to the peaceful society that G-d envisioned when He created man.

2) ***Eidos.*** These laws increase man's awareness of G-d and His deeds. They testify to G-d's control over the world. Their purpose is to lift man to a higher spiritual level and to prod him to a purer, holier life. Examples of *Eidos* include the observance of the *Shabbos,* and the Jewish holidays, and the use of such symbolic articles as *Tefillin, Tzitzis,* and *Mezuzah*—reminders of G-d's presence.

By helping man feel closer to G-d, these laws evoke his potential for righteousness. One who shares in the spirituality of *Shabbos* will not be mired in the rut of the rat race. He will realize that there is more to life than eating, sleeping, and worrying about money. *Shabbos* and *Yom Tov* allow man more time to spend with his family. They help him feel closer to his fellow Jews, who celebrate identical commemorations of Jewish survival. The *Eidos* elevate a man's soul, and remind him that he is part of the Jewish nation—one of a comforting whole.

3) ***Chukim***. These laws, such as *sha'atnez* (not wearing wool and linen mixed together in the same garment) and not eating milk and meat products together, are perhaps the most difficult of all

Jewish laws to accept. This is because the Torah gives no specific reasons for them. Various possible rationales for them have been offered by the Sages. (For instance, the ban on mixing wool and linen or milk and meat may symbolize the need to separate intrinsically different items or acts.) It might also be said that these laws test man's self-discipline and the extent of his faith in G-d. Whatever the reason, G-d saw fit to promulgate these laws in His infinite wisdom. Man may not be on a sufficiently high spiritual or intellectual level to understand them fully, which is perhaps why G-d did not reveal their reasons.(This is similar to a doctor not fully explaining the causes of a diet to a patient who won't comprehend them. G-d puts man on a diet too—a spiritual one—and man can't totally understand the spiritual needs of his body). Because these are G-d's commands, it is up to man to accept His judgment and comply with it. This is in itself a lesson—not that we must always comply with every law legislated by every authority, but that sometimes we must restrict our impulses even when we are not told why. When a parent asks a child to do something which the child may not like or understand at first, though it is in the child's best interests (such as giving up television viewing for some studying), the child should still comply. True, a parent is human, and can be wrong. But G-d is beyond the realm of error. His laws are perfect, because He is perfect. Why should man take the chance of disregarding the *Chukim* and failing G-d's test of will-power, when he might eventually suffer for it? Rather, man should obey G-d's laws even if he does not always understand their purpose. This is the concept of *Emunah*—total faith in G-d's wisdom, under all conditions.

The laws of Judaism, then, have a variety of purposes:

a) They ensure man's recogniton of G-d, and his willingness to place complete faith in Him.

b) They help man live a pure, decent life and curb his baser instincts.

c) They influence man to treat his fellow man justly and kindly.

d) They remind him that he is a member of the Jewish nation, and that he has to set an exemplary example for others.

e) They provide spiritual nourishment for his soul in a manner similar to foods providing physical nourishment for the body.

A truly observant Jew must exhibit many outstanding personal qualities. He should show a special concern for others' welfare, going out of his way to help the needy. He should avoid any act that might cause physical, monetary, or psychological harm to his fellow man; and must therefore, watch his deeds and his comments very carefully. He must always be aware of G-d's presence, and should remember that lying and cheating can only harm him. Even if no one else catches him in the act, G-d will. He should lead a decent, family-oriented life, setting a proper moral example for his children and for his neighbors. His lifestyle should so impress others that even non-Jews will admire the Jewish way of life. One who lives up to these standards, is indeed a good Jew.

Question Twenty One: Why, then, are there some Jews who claim to be observant but do not have all of these admirable qualities?

Answer: If a house collapses, this does not mean that its blueprint was faulty. The problem may stem from its construction.

The same is true of a Jew who goes wrong. His blueprint for living—the Holy Torah— is faultless. If all men lived up to its laws and its guiding spirit, model societies would arise.

The fact that some who call themselves observant Jews act improperly indicates problems with the person, not with the Torah. In short, the person is not living up to the high ideals of the Torah. All individuals are prone to error. Observant Jews can also fall prey to the impulses of the *Yetzer Ho'Rah*: pride, greed, envy, hate. Perhaps they experienced difficult childhoods, or incomplete educational training. Perhaps they are not as friendly to others as they should be—not as ready to show kindness to fellow humans as they are to show allegiance to G-d. Perhaps it is sometimes easier to be more faithful to the letter of the law than to its spirit.

However, there is no excuse for such behavior. Those who present themselves as Orthodox Jews to the world have a special obligation to create a positive image of themselves for others. They must go out of their way to perform acts of kindness, and to avoid corruption and greed. After all, the world will judge Jews on the basis of their behavior. If they are seen as aloof or conniving, the enemies of the Jews will gloat. They will serve as proof for those who downplay religion. There could be no worse example of *Chilul Hashem*—a profanation of G-d's name.

Question Twenty Two: Aren't Jewish laws restrictive? Don't they limit one's enjoyment of life?

Answer: Yes, many laws of Judaism are restrictive; almost all laws are. They are restrictive in that they try to make man avoid doing today what he might be sorry for tomorrow. A person may enjoy an alcoholic "high" for the moment, but a hangover will soon follow. Judaism aims to remove the hangover of decadence by removing the decadence itself. A person can remain spiritually and morally pure only if he restricts his activities. This is why Judaism asks the Jew to restrict his diet, his mode of dress, his actions on *Shabbos* and holidays, his relations with the opposite sex, and his tendency to abuse the rights of others. The goal is not to make man miserable, but to elevate his happiness to a higher plane. There is more lasting joy in a close and sincere relationship with a spouse than there is in a casual encounter. There is more spiritual glow in a *Shabbos* experience than there is in a drug fix.

Some might protest that absolute freedom is absolutely necessary. This might sound fine in theory, but in practice it is not feasible. Absolute freedom allows everyone to satisfy his own personal aims, even if this means trampling on the rights of others. Absolute freedom can carry with it waves of murders, robberies, and rapes—of crumbling families and deteriorating societies. Absolute freedom allows a person to destroy his body with excess food and drugs. Clearly, some restrictions are needed, for man's own good. This is why Judaism limits the harmful impulses of man: to let his good nature emerge.

However, one should not make the mistake of thinking that Judaism favors asceticism—hardship for hardship's sake. In fact, Judaism totally rejects the idea that man exists on earth to suffer, and that he must deny himself all pleasures. On the contrary, Judaism believes that the pleasures of the world were created for man to enjoy, and that when one rejects all such pleasures, he rejects G-d's goodness. This is why Judaism encourages its members to joyously celebrate many holidays, complete with feasting and song. It advises its members to dress well, eat nutritiously, and live comfortably. It instructs its adherents not to withdraw from the world, but to take part in it—to marry and have children (an exhortation applying to its priests—the *Kohanim*—as well). "*Ivdu Es Hashem B'Simcha*"—Serve G-d Through Joy—is a basic tenet of Judaism. Anyone who has been to a Purim celebration, or to a Jewish wedding, or to a "*farbrengin*", or to a "Yeshivishe" gathering, knows the extent of the happiness that Jews can experience. Jewish song, humor, and cuisine are well-known and are enjoyed even by non-Jews. Indeed, religious Jews are to be found participating in most aspects of life today. But they always avoid the seamy side, remembering that their task in life is to retain the spark of holiness that G-d gave them.

While allowing Jews to share in the joys of life, Judaism cautions against hedonism and materialism. Jews are reminded that they are not on this earth *solely* to gain pleasure and possessions. In fact, the pressure to gain material wealth, to keep on an even par with the rich neighbors, and to protect one's wealth from robbers or the tax man is enough to give even the calmest of men ulcers. True, there might be a momentary pleasure in having expensive goods, or in drink, drugs, and debauchery, but this is only superficial, temporary happiness. What is left when that moment of good feeling has flown? What is left when you're middle aged and worn out? What is left when you die? How can those few moments of joy compensate for the terror of desperately seeking another drug fix, or of dying for another drink or of facing death and expecting the worst in the World to Come?

What Judaism encourages is a balanced life. Don't deny yourself the pleasures of the world, but don't go overboard and lose your self-control. Enjoy food and celebrations, but don't gorge yourself. Strive for the long-lasting happiness that goes with a stable family, a non-pressured life style, and a steady devotion to G-d. Experience the enduring satisfaction of being a full-fledged member of the Jewish people, knowing who you are and whom you can depend on for help. Gain the peace of mind that comes with realizing that this is only a temporary world, and that you have rewards to look forward to in the World to Come.

This is the ideal existence. It can come only within the structured, restrictive framework of Torah laws.

Question Twenty-Three: Aren't many of the Torah laws old-fashioned and meant for an earlier civilization? How can one possibly be an observant Jew and still fit into today's modern world?

Answer: The terms "modern" and "old-fashioned" are extremely relative ones.

What is considered modern today can easily turn old-fashioned by tomorrow; what seems passé today can emerge as tomorrow's nostalgic craze. One doesn't have to be an historian to realize how rapidly man changes his clothing fashions, his hair styles, his modes of entertainment, his values and interests. If Judaism were to alter its laws to accommodate every change in public taste, it would hardly be a stable religion. Its adherents could never be sure whether a certain law was "in" or "out" that week.

Judaism's basic laws deal with man's eternal condition. There is nothing old-fashioned about such admonitions as "Honor Your Parents" or "You Shall Not Kill." They are as valid today as when G-d gave them to Moshe Rabbeinu thousands of years ago. The *Mishpotim*—the laws to improve man's relations with his fellow men—are certainly still relevant. The poor and the sick are still part of the world's population, and are as much in need of assistance as ever. We must still be reminded to love others as we would ourselves and to avoid slandering or injuring our neighbors. With crime statistics more depressing than ever, we must still be told to forsake murder, cheating, and robbery. There is nothing outdated about such laws.

Neither are Jewish holidays irrelevant today. Through them, we relive glorious moments in the history of the Jews. By celebrating *Pesach, Succos, Purim, Chanukah,* and other such holidays, we join with other Jews in showing our pride at being Jewish. And, with the impersonality of the modern world, and today's "lonely crowd", our need for a personal, caring G-d has never been greater. Therefore, the chance to come closer to G-d through prayer and *Shabbos* observance is still vital.

Of course, new discoveries and technologies have created a world that *is* different from the one that saw the giving of the Torah. Certain Torah laws, particularly those relating to the *Beis Hamikdosh,* are not applicable at this time. Other Torah laws have been shown by learned Sages to apply to new conditions, such as the use of electricity. The Rabbis rely on decisions of their predecessors to render opinions in new situations—just as, *l'havdil,* secular courts rely on precedents from earlier courts when they hand down their decisions. The Rabbis remain a living, dynamic link to the law codes of the past, expounding the Torah's view on modern-day cases while remaining faithful to the age-old ideals of G-d. They enable Judaism to withstand the challenges of any age.

What is incredible is the way in which Judaism has thrived in so many different nations and cultures throughout the years—not only in Eretz Yisroel, but also in Babylonia, Spain, Morocco, Poland, Rumania, Hungary, Russia, Western Europe, South America, Canada, and the United States. The Jews in each country managed to become respectable, law-abiding citizens, but their first allegiance was reserved for their religion. They survived as Jews because they adapted the culture around them to fit Judaism, not the reverse. The basic laws and ideals of Judaism have proved sufficiently timeless and universal to be able to take root in many different societies during many different eras. There is no need to change them.

There is no question that one can be an observant Jew and a full participant in today's world, especially in the United States. *Yeshivos* are available to provide Jewish youngsters with both a solid training in Judaism and a fully-rounded secular education. Camping and physical education programs, under Jewish auspices, allows them to become physically fit and athletically adept. Orthodox Jews have no trouble entering colleges or vocational programs. They have gained many high-ranking positions in the best of companies. Jewish organizations have fought for laws to make sure that Orthodox employees need not work on *Shabbos* or Jewish holidays. (In fact, few businesses now operate on Saturdays, and many—including government agencies—allow for vacations on religious holidays, as do many schools and colleges.) Kosher foods have become easily obtainable and identifiable, and violators of *Kashrus* codes are punished by the governments of many states. Jewish organizations today also help train Jews for jobs, give services to the needy and elderly, and allow new immigrants to adjust to new lives as Jews in a new country. The laws of the land prohibit discrimination on the basis of religion alone. Though there might be some difficulties, there are no major obstacles in the way of one who wants to be both religious and successful in society. A little effort can gain both goals.

Question Twenty-Four: Why can't Judaism allow for more democracy in determining laws? Why can't each man on his own decide how to live properly?

Answer: It might seem simple for one to be able to decide what is right and what is wrong, and to act accordingly. However, the definition of right and wrong, of good and bad, has eluded philosophers throughout history. What might seem good to one individual might prove harmful to another. For instance, someone might decide that it is morally correct for all men to have equal wealth. He might therefore consider it a logical consequence to steal money from someone else—after all, why should the other person have more than he? The fact that the other person worked hard to obtain that extra money may not concern him. Or someone might consider himself a perfectly decent and ethical person if he simply does not cause any harm to anyone else—but at the same time, he might not feel compelled to give charity to the poor or comfort to the needy. No doubt some Nazis thought that they were acting in the best interests of their countrymen when they began their campaign to rid the world of Jews. So how can man, with his subjective viewpoint and personal bias, be asked to decide what is right and what is wrong? As we mentioned at the very beginning, man's thinking is limited.

The task of defining good and bad is left to One Who does not have human flaws and Who is above selfish gains: G-d. His Torah is the one authentic source for knowledge of right and wrong, for good and bad. Without the Torah providing these guidelines, man would be left to the chaos of his own subjective decisions. The world has seen too many examples of totalitarian leaders telling the populace that whatever they do is good. It has seen too many misguided individuals taking the law into their own hands at someone else's expense. It is up to the Jews to show the world that active concern for one's fellow man, control of one's destructive impulses, and striving for sanctity of life all lead to a truly ethical existence.

It can also be asked why the common man can't interpret Torah law instead of the Rabbis and Sages. The answer is that only the Rabbis, through their extensive study of the Torah, have obtained a thorough knowledge of the intricacies of the law. In a similar way, a graduate of law school is more qualified than the average layman to adjudicate court cases. The field of *Rabbonus,* it should be noted, is open to all, regardless of wealth and heritage. And even the layman should gain a solid grasp of fundamental Jewish law, so that he can deal with basic *halachic* questions as best he can on his own. If he has any doubts about Jewish law in any specific case, he should by all means consult a reliable Rabbi.

Question Twenty-Five: If Torah law is supreme, why have some Jews formed separate branches of Judaism which seek to update the Torah?

Answer: The Torah describes the Jews as a "stiff-necked" people. Throughout history many Jews have tried to rebel against the *Torah* and the religious status quo. As mentioned before, numerous groups tried to establish themselves as alternatives to Torah-true Judaism. Most have since faded from view.

The combined forces of the Industrial and Scientific Revolutions led to another such effort. Reform Judaism developed in Germany and Russia as part of the *Haskoloh* (Enlightenment) movement of the 1800's. This was an attempt to make Judaism appear as "modern" and "progressive" as possible, in an effort to gain full acceptance for Jews in gentile society. Along the way, the Reform movement abandoned almost all laws of the Torah, claiming that the Torah was not G-d-given. In their Pittsburgh Platform, Reform leaders downplayed Eretz Yisroel as the final destination of the Jews and rejected the idea of a personal Messiah, claiming instead that by living up to the general ethical standards of the Bible, man could establish a Messianic society wherever he was.

This almost total rejection of Judaism as a religion was too much for some Jews who nevertheless did not want to be traditional Jews. This group established Conservative Judaism, which feels that the Reform movement made too sharp a break with tradition, but that Judaism must still change with the times. Consequently, Conservative Jews conform to some laws, but not to others. Another, smaller break-away branch is Reconstructionism, which feels that Judaism is more a civilization and a culture than a religion.

One of the hopes of Reform Jews of the 1800's and early 1900's was that their compromising attitude toward religion would make them more acceptable to their gentile neighbors. Unfortunately, this did not exactly happen. Whatever gains they made were obliterated by the brutal Russian pogroms, and the horrors of the Holocaust. The gentiles showed that to them, Orthodox or Reform, a Jew was a Jew, to be reviled and rejected.

America, with its history of democracy, and permissiveness, proved more hospitable to the Reform notion of freedom in religion. Reform Jews went out of their way to play up their similarities to the gentiles and to play down any differences. They were so successful that their adherents soon noted no differences at all. Lately, even leaders of Reform Judaism have begun to notice the sweeping trend toward assimilation, intermarriage, and conversion in their ranks. American Jewry is fast fading away—and is it any wonder? Can a Jew whose Judaism is so watered down feel a staunch member of his religion? Why should he identify himself as a Jew when he does not know what it means to be a Jew? Why should he believe in a Bible that is supposedly man-made, and why should he believe in an impersonal G-d whose laws can be changed? Why should he accept a version of a religion that has nothing to do with tradition? For if the original form of the religion has no relevance to today's world, why bother with it at all?

Conservative Judaism may not be as bothered by these basic questions. Yet it faces an identity crisis. Just where does it stand? Does it truly believe in the authenticity of the Torah; and if so, why doesn't it follow it faithfully? Can G-d-given laws be changed for the convenience of one generation of man? If Conservative Judaism is neither fully traditional nor fully new, then what exactly is it?

Orthodox Judaism believes that the Torah was given directly by G-d to Moshe Rabbeinu. It therefore logically concludes that its laws are universally applicable and cannot be changed whenever man so desires. It also believes that a human Messiah will come to return the Jews to Eretz Yisroel, and that the righteous will gain further rewards in the World to Come. Orthodox Judaism faces no identity crisis. It is the same unadulterated form of Judaism that Jews observed from the time of Moshe on through the generations. An Orthodox Jew can cling to Judaism with the fervor of one who knows that he savors something authentic.

However, Orthodox Jews must realize that they cannot gain further adherents just by attacking non-observant Jews. There are many sincere, ethical, and well-meaning individuals with a strong Jewish conscience who have not adopted Orthodoxy because they feel it is too big a burden to bear, or because they can't relate to Orthodox Jews, or because they lack a good Jewish education and can't have any real appreciation for the eternal values of authentic Judaism. It is up to Orthodox Jews to take the initiative: to show his fellow, non-observant Jews that Orthodoxy is not too difficult—that it is synonymous with purity—with friendship, with happiness. He must show concern for the welfare of all other Jews, Orthodox or not, and must set the proper example that will win over others. Hillel used to advise others to be like Aharon—one who pursued peace and loved *all* mankind. More can be accomplished for Torah Judaism through love and kindness than through hate and condemnation.

Perhaps we can cherish the hope that all of Israel will one day again be united as full-fledged, Torah-true Jews.

SUMMARY OF PART THREE

Jewish laws are, as we have seen, vital to the survival of the Jewish people. They help curb man's natural destructive tenden-

cies, and lead him instead to the path of righteousness and self-control. Absolute freedom would be detrimental to the welfare of human societies, so laws have been instituted for the common good. It is only the purely objective, G-d-given Torah which can state which laws are good and right.

We have seen how the Jewish laws of the *Torah have been transmitted and applied to the present world by the Rabbis, who are the supreme judges of Jewish law by virtue of their knowledge. Orthodox Judaism believes that these laws are as relevant to today's society as they were in the time of Moshe Rabbeinu.*

Now that we have gained an overall view of the need for laws in general, let us examine the rationale behind some specific laws.

PART FOUR

EXPLORING SPECIFIC JEWISH LAWS

PART FOUR: EXPLORING SPECIFIC JEWISH LAWS

Question Twenty-Six: What might be the rationale behind Shabbos (the Sabbath) *and Yom Tov* (Jewish Holidays)*?*

Answer: The idea of a Sabbath—a day of rest—has by now become almost universally accepted. Its origin lies in the Torah tradition. The Torah states that, after the six days of creation, "G-d 'rested' from His work." Man is told to follow suit, in recognition of G-d's mastery over the world.

To some Jews, *Shabbos* has become just a day for escaping from the office to watch football games unfold on TV. Some might view *Shabbos* as a day of severe restrictions—a burden, a day when they are told not to carry, or write, or spend money, or watch television. Is *Shabbos,* then, intended just as a chance to catch up on sports or sleep? Does it exist to make life difficult and boring?

The answer is no. Those who perceive *Shabbos* in these terms do not understand its purposes. Chances are that they have also not experienced it properly. What, then is the real purpose of *Shabbos*?

As mentioned above, the seventh day of the week was the one on which G-d "rested" after He created the world. This statement presents an obvious problem. Did G-d, the All-Powerful Deity, really need a respite? Certainly not, or else he would not be G-d. Rather the Torah indicates that G-d "rested" in order to set an example for man to follow.

We read that G-d "labored" on the world for six days. Then he saw fit to cease creating new material, contrasting the limitations of the material world with the boundlessness of the spiritual one. It is in this sense that *Shabbos* allows man to emulate G-d: to stress spirituality over materialism.

For six days of the week, we concern ourselves with mundane matters: with business, schoolwork, shopping and entertainment. Sometimes we become so engrossed in our work that we become almost enslaved to it. The businessman who worries himself sick over a deal; the housewife who sizzles over a hot stove; the student who studies till dawn—all are in bondage to the dream of success. Man concentrates on materialistic goals—money, possessions, prestige, overlooking the more basic happiness that comes from a cohesive family, a solid friendship, and a sense of purity. In the bustle of day-to-day business, who has time to think of holiness, or of G-d?

Shabbos makes us pause in our weekly grind. It reminds us that we can transcend daily drudgery, that there is a spiritual light at the end of the week's tunnel. *Shabbos* replaces the everyday humdrum air with a special aura of holiness. *Shabbos* purifies us, strengthens our ties with others, and brings us closer to G-d.

This helps explain why we refrain from work on *Shabbos*. In the same sense that G-d stopped creating new material matter after six days, man halts his own materialistic creativity. Actually, the amount or the difficulty of the work is unimportant. What is forbidden is doing *"melochos."* These are positive, creative acts of the type performed in the *Mishkan* (Tabernacle) when the Jews were in the desert. Carrying heavy books inside the house is permitted, even though this might require much physical exertion. But carrying a book outside is forbidden, though it might not seem like work at all. This is because, by not doing *melochos*, we are reminded that on *Shabbos* man should not attempt to control the environment through constructive acts. *Shabbos* is a day for man to acknowledge G-d's supremacy over the world. *Shabbos* is a day for man to free himself from the worries and aches of his earthly labors, and to recall that, in the end, only his holy deeds are the ones that will count. *Shabbos* is a day not only for physical rest, but also for peace of mind.

But *Shabbos* is not a day of forced inactivity. On the contrary; *Shabbos* is an opportunity for great achievements. It is the perfect day for the family to finally come together after six days of varied locations and interests, to sit around the *Shabbos* table and enjoy each other's company. The *Shabbos* meal, complete with *Zemiros* (songs), *Divrei Torah*, and a relaxed atmosphere, provides a much better opportunity for a family interaction than does sitting around the TV set. Perhaps *Shabbos* is a major reason for the stability of the traditional Jewish household.

Shabbos also gives one a chance to improve his relationships with others. Here is one day on which we can visit neighbors and enjoy each other's company. It is a day on which many Jews invite Jews from other communities to their homes, to partake of the *Shabbos* meals and experience the warmth of Jewish hospitality. Jews who feel "out in the cold" can look forward to *Shabbos* as a day when they will not be alone. In this way, *Shabbos* cements bonds between Jews the world over.

Naturally, *Shabbos* also brings Jews closer to G-d. Dressed in fine clothing, eating specially prepared food, reciting special prayers, one feels the presence of the Deity more so than usual. And, of course, on *Shabbos* one has more time to devote to the study of the Torah and to a consideration of G-d's greatness. The special *Shabbos* spirit, the feeling that this is not just another ordinary day, can provide one with an extra lift that can carry him through the rest of the week, dreary as it may be.

Shabbos also provides for the spiritual regeneration of man through an actual infusion of new spirit, called *Neshomoh Yeseirah.*

Finally, *Shabbos* can help a person gain a clear perspective on his own self being. This is one day he does not have to worry about the demands of his employer or his teacher. On this day, free of all pressures, he can take stock of what he has accomplished, where he stands, and where he should be going. He can come to grips with himself, and can consider ways to improve himself. The day of rest is a day of introspection.

To sum up, *Shabbos* is a break in the weekly routine—a chance for man to remember that he is G-d's creation, with an obligation to care for his family, his fellow man, and himself. Rather than being a day of restrictions, *Shabbos* is a spiritual oasis in an earth-bound week.

The *Yomim Tovim*, the Jewish holidays, serve a similar function. They, too, elevate Jews from the ordinary to the special. Specifically, they are reminders of glorious moments in Jewish history. They commemorate miraculous events and spiritual triumphs. Sometimes they help us to reflect on our own past and to think of ways to make the future better.

The following section provides a synopsis of the Jewish holidays and their significance:

a) *Rosh Hashonah*—The beginning of the Jewish year ushers in a period of intense introspection—a realization that G-d's judgment of man is dependent on man's self-improvement. The stirring sounds of the *Shofar* (ram's horn), inspire man to make the coming year a better one.

b) *Yom Kippur*—The Day of Atonement is the climax of the Ten Days of Repentance that begin with *Rosh Hashonah. Yom Kippur* is a day when man goes without food and without work, free to concentrate on communications with G-d and on self-defects that can be corrected. *Yom Kippur* marks the cleansing of the soul.

c) *Succos*—This is a joyous holiday, recalling the survival of the Jews during their stay in the desert. We commemorate this by eating in *Succohs* (huts) like those that sheltered the Jews during their wandering. They are reminders of the precarious existence of the Jews, who are dependent on G-d for their safety. *Succos* is also the time when we take the *Lulov* and *Esrog*—symbols of the unity of the Jewish people and reminders of the harvest season in Eretz Yisroel—and it culminates in *Simchas Torah,* when we rejoice at the conclusion and the renewal of the weekly Torah reading.

d) *Chanukah*—This holiday celebrates a double triumph: the miraculous victory of the *Chashmonoim* led by Yehuda HaMaccabee over the (Syrian) Greeks, and the miraculous find of pure oil for the Menorah in the *Beis Hamikdosh,* oil which lasted for eight days. The latter is the cause for the daily lighting of the *Menorah* during each of the eight days of *Chanukah.*

e) *Tu B'Shvat*—This "New Year for Trees" in Eretz Yisroel gives man an opportunity to thank G-d for the blessings of nature and to ask for a fruitful harvest season ahead.

f) *Purim*—This celebrates the failure of Haman's diabolical scheme to destroy the Jews of the Persian Empire, thanks to the efforts of Queen Esther and Mordechai. The reading of the *Megillah,* as well as special feasts and masquerades, mark the Jews' salvation in Shushan.

g) *Pesach*—G-d's deliverance of the Jews from their bondage in Egypt is the basis for this holiday. No bread is eaten during that time, as a reminder of the hasty departure of the Jews from their slavery. *The Pesach Seder* is a ceremonial meal during which this redemption is symbolically recalled.

h) *Shevuos*—On this day, the Jews received the Torah at Mt. Sinai, signifying their emergence as G-d's Chosen People.

i) *Tisha B'Av*—This is a national day of mourning, a day on which no food is eaten, in memory of the two Holy Temples—the *Botei Mikdosh*—which were destroyed on this day.

It should be noted that there are other commemorations and fast days; and that Jews outside of Israel add an extra day to some holidays (like *Succos, Pesach,* and *Shevuos*). This is because centuries ago, the exact date of the new month depended on witnesses testifying in Jerusalem about the moon's position. (The Hebrew year is based on lunar calculations.) It took time for word of this testimony to reach distant lands, so those there added a day to *Yom Tov* as a precaution. We maintain this tradition to this very day.

The *Yomim Tovim* remind Jews of their heritage and nationality. They give Jews a cause for common celebration, and provide a spiritual uplift that helps them face harsh times and hostile conditions.

Observing *Shabbos* and *Yom Tov* has been made easier in recent years by government laws protecting Jews against discrimination if they are faithful to their traditions. It is certainly not an overwhelming hardship for one to keep these traditions. On the contrary: without them, the Jewish spirit would suffer.

Question Twenty-Seven: What might be the rationale of Kashrus (Kosher foods)?

Answer: Let us first explain what is meant by *Kashrus*. There are several categories of Kosher foods, including:

a) The restriction against eating the meat of animals that do not have fully cloven hooves and which do not chew their cud; the eating of fish that do not have fins and scales; and the eating of various birds, especially those that are notably predatory. Animals that do not have Kosher characteristics are called *treif* or *tomeih* (impure), and neither they nor their by-products can be eaten. Examples of non-Kosher foods include pork, lobsters, snails and many kinds of gelatin and shortening.

b) The restriction against eating the meat of a Kosher animal that has not undergone *Shechita* before its death. *Shechita* is a specialized process of killing the animal with a knife in a humane way. The animal is thoroughly inspected before undergoing *Shechita,* to make sure that it contains no grave wounds. The carcasses of animals which died before undergoing *Shechita* cannot be eaten. Poultry must also undergo special preparation before being considered Kosher.

c) The restriction against cooking or eating dairy and meat products together. After one has eaten a meat food, one must wait several hours before eating a dairy food (though the reverse is not true). For this reason, Jews keep separate *milchig* (dairy) and *fleishig* (meat) cooking utensils and dinnerware.

Some assume that the sole basis for *Kashrus* is one of health or sanitary considerations. They feel that *Kashrus* originated to prevent Jews from contracting certain diseases (such as trichinosis from pig meat), but now that these diseases can be avoided by other means, the laws of *Kashrus* are no longer valid. This is not the case. Although *Kashrus* does promote good health, digestion, and cleanliness, these are not its only rationales.

Among the additional reasons for *Kashrus* are the following:

a) **Promoting the Purity of Man**: There is an old observation that "you are what you eat." This does not, of course, mean that man turns into his own dinner. Rather, it suggests that man's eating habits indicate and influence his personality. Consider this picture: Someone tears off the limbs of a dead animal with his bare hands, sinks his teeth into as large a hunk of meat as possible, and then belches heartily afterwards, with blood gushing all around him. Not a very appetizing sight, is it? This is the way an animal in the wild eats. No doubt the glutton who follows this example is a barbarous animal himself. On the other hand, consider someone savoring a delicacy with the finesse of a gourmet, exhibiting perfect table manners throughout. This is the mark of a civilized person. The Jew is told to eat in a civilized manner, in a way that shows his noble heritage. He is told to keep his body as pure as he keeps his soul, by controlling what foods enter it.

The Jew is therefore careful to avoid animals that represent bloodshed, such as the lion, the vulture, and the shark; and to avoid animals that are dirty, diseased, and repulsive, such as the pig, the insect, and bloody carcass. By keeping away from them, he remembers to reject their savage lifestyles. By eating only foods of a benign nature—milk products, fruits, vegetables, produces from domesticated animals like cows and chickens—he retains the purity of his Divinely-given body. By following the cleanliness *Kashrus* promotes, man feels more like an angel than a slob after a meal. He is reminded that he is not a wild animal scrounging for prey, but a Divine creation with a Divine spark.

b) **Promoting Self Control**: As was mentioned before, man is subject to whims and impulses, some of which are destructive and must therefore be controlled. He must learn that he cannot get everything he wants exactly when he wants. If he did, he would probably be harming someone else. *Kashrus* is also an exercise in self-control. Jews who eat only Kosher food learn that they cannot satisfy their hunger in every way they might want. They learn to restrict themselves to foods approved by G-d, for the reasons mentioned above. They learn that certain things have different natures and should not be mixed, like meat and milk. They learn to be selective in what they allow inside their bodies, as they must be selective in their actions.

c) **Promoting Humaneness:** The process of *Shechita* is designed to make the death of the animal as painless as possible. The slaughtering must take place quickly, and the knife used must be free of any nicks which might make the animal suffer. All death is instantaneous, and prolonged suffering is avoided. All this is designed to show man that, though animals serve man's needs, they are also creations of G-d. Man must therefore treat them as humanely as possible. For the same reason, Judaism forbids *Eiver Min Ha'Chai* (eating the limb of a live animal), and discourages hunting for sport. If man learns to treat animals kindly, he should come to treat his fellow man with at least as much respect.

d) **Promoting Jewish Unity**: A Jew must search for stores and homes that sell and serve Kosher food. Of course, most such places are owned by Jews. In this way, Jews tend to meet and support other Jews. A Jewish visitor in a strange town eats his meals in a local Jewish home, thereby strengthening his ties to Judaism. And the Jewish farmer, butcher, and grocer earn a livelihood with the help of Jewish customers.

In recent years, the observance of *Kashrus* has been made easier, especially in the United States. Many food manufacturers have accepted Rabbinical supervision of their products. Certification of *Kashrus* is easily identifiable on packages of food. In addition, many new ingredients have been developed to allow Jews to substitute kosher and pareve foods for non-kosher, dairy and meat ones. So Jews who observe *Kashrus* can do so in relative ease, and can enjoy a wide variety of tasty and nutritious foods.

Question Twenty-Eight: *What is the purpose of Tefilloh, Tefillin, Tzitzis, Yarmulkeh, and Mezuzah?*

Answer: Jews pray three times a day—*Shacharis* (in the morning), *Mincha* (in the afternoon), and *Maariv* (in the evening), and say additional prayers on special occasions. They also recite blessings (*Berochos*) at certain times, such as before and after eating. Male Jews wear *Tzitzis* and *Talleisim* (garments containing specially designed strings), as well as a head covering called a *Yarmulkeh,* and, during the morning prayers, *Tefillin* (Phylacteries) on the arm and head. Every Jewish household has a *Mezuzah*—a small container with a parchment of the *Shema* prayer—affixed to the right doorposts of their dwellings.

What lessons do these teach us?

Let us examine each in turn.

a) **Tefilloh.** Communication is a key element of our generation. We have developed technology that lets man converse with others thousands of miles away; we can dispatch messages that will be received in minutes. Yet, man still has trouble communicating. Parents and children, husbands and wives, employers and employees have difficulty expressing themselves clearly to each other. The so-called "communications gap" can prove most frustrating.

If man has so much trouble communicating with his fellow man, imagine how hard it is for him to communicate with G-d.

Tefilloh helps bridge this gap.

Man has much to say to G-d. He can thank G-d for showing him favor, or he can ask G-d for special kindness, or he can beseech G-d for the good health of a dear one. He may want to express his feelings and fears and pledges of repentance; he may want to voice his awe of and love for the Almighty. How can he do so?

In the time of the *Mishkon* and the *Beis Hamikdosh,* he could bring a sacrifice to atone for sins or to show his appreciation for a favor as well as having to pray. The *Beis Hamikdosh* is no longer standing, but man can still reach G-d through prayer. *Tefillos* are a direct link to G-d. No intermediaries are needed. After one has prayed with full devotion (*kavonah*), he feels cleansed, purified. He has communicated with the Almighty, and he knows that his prayers stand a chance of being answered.

Prayer is especially effective in times of crisis. When a loved one is sick, or when one's fortunes seem bleak, and one can do nothing to relieve the situation, he can still pray. It is always a source of solace.

Traditional *Tefillos* are in Hebrew. This is because it is the *Loshon Hakodesh*—the original, holy language of the men of the Torah—which is more pleasing to G-d. Hebrew *Tefillos* also unify the Jews: Jews who come from different countries and who speak different languages can still pray together without any barriers between them. At the same time, one should understand what he says when he prays, and prayers in any language are accepted by G-d if they are truly heartfelt.

Jews come together to the *Beis Haknesses* (synagogue) to pray together, preferably in a *Minyan* (an assembly of ten or more men over the age of 13). This *Tefillah B'Tzibbur* brings the Jews together, and strengthens their sense of community while making their common plea more effective. The *Beis Haknesses* is a holy place, and it is more than just a brick building. It is a place of warmth and brotherhood, where Jews both young and old find a common bond.

Tefilloh, then, enables man to speak directly to G-d, and to assemble with his fellow Jews in a common cause.

b) **Tzitzis and Tefillin** are symbols. The Torah stipulated their use to remind Jews of their allegiance to G-d and His *Mitzvos.* One who looks at the *Tzitzis* (such as during the recitation of the *Shema* prayer) remembers that he must perform the 613 *Torah Mitzvos.* (The letters of the word "*Tzitzis*" in Hebrew have the numerical value of 600; this is added to the five knots and eight strings of the *Tzitzis* to equal 613). The *Tefillin* contain various sections of the *Shema* and other parts of the *Torah* written on parchment. The placement of the *Tefillin* on the head and the arm (opposite the heart) symbolically represents the fact that man must serve G-d through his actions, feelings, and thoughts. The *Tzitzis* and *Tefillin* are holy artifacts that constantly remind man, through their symbolism, that he must make a special effort to live up to Torah standards.

c) **Yarmulkeh.** The term "*yarmulkeh*" is a contraction of the words "*yorei malkah*"—fear of the Heavenly King. When one wears a head covering, he displays a respect for G-d. He shows that he is aware that there is a Being above him, and that he cannot walk around brazenly bareheaded, as if he was master of the world. The *yarmulkeh* is a sign of respect, and that is why it should be worn at all times.

In addition, the *yarmulkeh* is an identifying sign for Jews. One who wears a *yarmulkeh* in public is openly proclaiming that he is a Jew, and that he is proud to show it. The *yarmulkeh* shows Jews and non-Jews alike just how a person chooses to identify himself.

d) **Mezuzah.** The *Mezuzah* is also a symbolic item. Its presence on one's doorpost symbolizes the fact that G-d stands at the door to protect the Jewish abode as he did during the plagues in Egypt. It adds sanctity to that most important of places—the Jewish home.

Here, too, the *Mezuzah* allows one to openly identify himself as a Jew. One who sees a house or apartment with a *Mezuzah* affixed to its doorpost, can be sure a Jewish family lives there, and that the residents are not ashamed to let the world know it.

Question Twenty-Nine: How does Judaism view relations between the sexes?

Answer: Judaism does not consider sex a necessary evil. It does not tell its priests to abstain from marital relations. Rather, it views sex as one of G-d's gifts to man. However, like all treasures, sex should not be misused.

The primary purpose of sex is to enable the human race to reproduce. But while G-d wants man to propagate, He also wants man to live a decent, morally pure life—a life that is not animalistic. Animals also have sex drives, but they exercise no self-control over them. Man should rise above this submission to instinct, and should not act upon every sexual instinct he feels. One who gives in to every impulse has no real free will. He is just as limited as an animal.

The social reasons for self-control here are numerous. Sexual compatibility is just one ingredient in a stable marriage. Lasting love, mutual respect and affection, and common interests are also pillars on which successful marriages are based. If a couple is able to share all of these gifts, then their pairing will survive the small squabbles that come with living together. They will stay together because they share an emotional as well as a physical attachment. Therefore, their children will grow up in a secure environment of a stable family life—something that is all too rare nowadays. They will have the benefit of strong parental models guiding them, enabling them to move through childhood and adolescence with greater confidence. The care which Jewish men and women take to find mates, helps explain the relatively low rate of divorce among observant Jews. The sexual self-control limits breakups due to infidelity. The benefit is shared by both parents and their children—who will in turn tend to be good parents to their own children.

On the other hand, consider a couple who live together because of sexual attraction alone. They are interested in the thrills and sensations of the moment. They may get married, or (just as possibly, nowadays) they may not. In any case, the chances that they will stay together for long are not too good. Once they grow older and less physically attractive, they are apt to split, because there are no other ties holding them together. One of the results of "free sex" is that when you grow tired of someone, you simply move on to someone else. Without the legality of marriage, a relationship can be very tenuous. At the first argument, the partnership ends. And where does this leave a "sexually liberated" person at middle age? Often alone, emotionally worn out, and no longer attractive. This is not a very bright prospect to look forward to, especially at a time when man is living longer.

What if this sort of partnership has led to the birth of a child? How many teenagers are having babies without being able to properly care for them? What becomes of children from divorced and single-parent families? They often grow up feeling unloved, abandoned, uncared for, without proper parental models. They are more prone to emotional problems, to associations with drugs and crime. These are the prices paid for their parents' lack of foresight.

Judaism, on the other hand, sees the family unit as the cornerstone of the Jewish people, the basic structure protecting its existence. A strong family helps all its members weather the tempests of life. A stable home guarantees the transmission of Jewish tradition. A family rent by infidelity and incompatibility benefits no one.

Judaism therefore encourages individuals to restrain their powerful sex drives and choose marriage partners on the basis of many criteria. Once married, the husband and wife should be faithful to each other. This helps lead to secure family lives, and emotionally stable children.

In addition to causing failed marriage, sexual promiscuity can result in other major problems. Rape, venereal disease and prostitution are several obvious examples.

Because sex is such a strong drive, Judaism takes precautions against situations that might weaken one's self-control. This is why unmarried men and women are told not to stay alone together. It is why men and women are separated by a *mechitza* (partition) in the *Beis Haknesses*. After all, one's attention should be on one's prayers rather than on the opposite sex. It explains why Judaism has laws regarding *Niddah* and *Tzennius* (sexual modesty).

Demureness and restraint are the hallmark of the pure Jew.

Therefore by asking Jews to leash their impulses, Judaism seeks not to make life gloomy, but to render it as pure and stable as possible.

Question Thirty: *What is the role of the Jewish woman within Judaism? Do Torah laws discriminate against women?*

Answer: It is quite obvious that both men and women are indispensible if the world is to function successfully. The same is true of the Jewish world. Without the Jewish man and the Jewish woman both contributing to ongoing Jewish life, Judaism would suffer.

The Jewish woman is essential to Judaism in many ways. This is clearly seen from the examples of the many women who have played major roles in Jewish history. They include Sarah, whose sense of prophecy was even greater than her husband Abraham's; Rivkah, whose insights into her sons' natures were more penetrating than her husband Yitzchok's; Rachel and Leah who were the mothers of the tribes of Israel; the women of the *Midbar* (desert), who offered their jewels for use in the Mishkan; Chana, the selfless mother of Shmuel the Prophet; Chulda the Prophetess; Ruth, whose fidelity to Judaism led to the dynasty of her great-grandson, King David; Chana, who sacrificed her life rather than serve idols; Yael, who beheaded the enemy general Sisera; and Esther, the queen who saved her fellow Jews. The list of the devout women of all ages who practiced Judaism fervently and selflessly, and who aided and inspired those who knew them, is endless.

At the same time, it must be recognized that there are indeed differences between men and women. The most obvious one is the fact that it is the woman and not the man who becomes pregnant and bears the child. It is at this time that a woman can particularly use her husband's help and support. It has also been said that, in general terms, men are more capable of brute force than women, and that women show a greater sensitivity and sharper common sense than men—though, of course, this is not true in all cases.

The Torah nowhere implies that women are in any way inferior to men in intellect or natural abilities. There is no reason to believe that a woman could not perform the functions of President, Senator, Governor or corporation head as capably or even more capably than a man. Nor is there any reason why women who perform the exact same jobs as men should not receive equal pay. And Judaism severely condemns the exploitation of women as sex objects, or the stereotyping of women as a group rather than as individuals.

However, because of their physical and perhaps psychological differences, men and women can often best serve G-d in different ways.

For instance, as mentioned before, it is the woman who bears the child and who is usually more capable of rearing the baby (though the husband's involvement here is certainly necessary). The woman, who has the means to feed the baby and often feels that it has been a part of her, tends to show a greater sensitivity to its needs. Child rearing is certainly one of the most—if not *the* most—crucial tasks within the Jewish world, as it is in any society. If children are not raised with proper attention, love, understanding and religious and social guidance, they will develop problems. The mother, with her great capacity for understanding and affection, is especially equipped for this task. According to Jewish law, the decision of whether or not a child is Jewish is based on the religious identity of the mother, not the father. The mother therefore plays a pivotal role in the success of the Jewish family, and Jewish mothers have proven to be the key element in the survival of the family despite centuries of great struggle.

Recognizing this, Jewish law has given women dominance over the homefront, while giving men prominence in the public arena. Because the woman is so needed in managing the household, it is she who is assigned many of the *Mitzvos* associated with the home, such as the lighting of the *Shabbos* candles and the taking of the *Challah* portion of the dough. On the other hand, the man is given many of the *Mitzvos* relating to public life, such as *Tefillah*

B'Tzibbur, Rabbinical officiation, and testifying in public court. The fact that there might be more public than household *Mitzvos* does not mean that one domain is superior to the other. Again, the efforts of both men and women are equally essential for the preservation of Judaism.

Some point to the daily blessing "Blessed be You, O G-d . . . Who did not make me a woman," as evidence that Judaism considers women inferior. This is not true. The blessing refers to the fact that men are obligated to perform more *Mitzvos* than women, and therefore thank G-d for this extra opportunity. Men are expected to do more *Mitzvos* because women are free of all *Mitzvos* dependent on time (*Mitzvos Assai She'zeman Gerama*), such as *Tallis, Tefillin,* and certain holiday-related acts. The Torah did not want to force women to go to the *Beis Haknesses* or the *Beis Hamedrash* to pray and learn at length each day. If this were required of them, too, who would care for the children, and who would supervise the house? (Another possible reason for women's exclusion from these *Mitzvos* is that women are generally more secluded from the negative influences of society, and are on a higher spiritual level, having a greater role in the G-dly act of creation through giving birth. Men having more association with the outside world, are more likely to come into contact with negative influences, and therefore need the reminder of these *Mitzvos* to keep them constantly aware of G-d's supremacy.) Exclusion from these *Mitzvos* gives the woman more time to attend to important matters at home (and, perhaps, at work, too). This is not a punishment but an opportunity.

It should also be pointed out that Jewish wives are definitely not considered chattel. The Jewish wife has long enjoyed benefits that until recently were denied wives in other cultures. Under the Jewish marriage contract, the husband is obligated to provide for her support, her protection, and her happiness. He is prohibited from philandering and from causing her any harm. Consequently, divorces—though possible—are not that common among Orthodox Jews; and wife beating—still on the rise today in the most "civilized" societies—are rare. In the case of divorce, the husband must see to it that his ex-wife remains financially secure. The wife is therefore not treated as a slave, but rather as a privileged partner in the marriage.

In recent years, the role of the woman has been questioned and challenged. Many have rebelled against the sterotyped image of the woman as being a passive and underachieving fixture of the house. Unquestionably, the contributions and all-around talents of women have been downgraded during the years, and inequality persists. The notion that women can contribute their professsional talents to better the world should be supported. But the importance of the woman's role as wife and mother should not be forgotten, either. If all women start competing with men for control of the family and of society, the results would be damaging for both. Marriages would turn into battles of one-upmanship, with each partner trying to show that he or she is the superior partner. If neither parent is willing to "stoop" to the tasks of child rearing, what will become of the children? Not only won't they receive enough attention and guidance, but they will also become extremely confused as to their own sex roles. Jewish women must remember that, in the drive for women's rights, they must not relinquish the modesty that is expected of all Jews.

To summarize, then, the Torah certainly recognizes the central role played by women in passing on Jewish values and customs. It especially appreciates the capabilities of women in raising Jewish children. Therefore, women are exempted from certain specialized *Mitzvos* to allow them sufficient time for their vitally important activities. This does not mean, though, that women are second-class Jewish citizens. On the contrary, they are essential partners in the maintenance of the Jewish nation.

Question Thirty-One: What is the explanation of Jewish burial and mourning rites?

Answer: In Jewish thought, death is not an end, but a beginning. Judaism views this world like a waiting room, a preparation for the World to Come. This future world cannot be fully comprehended while man's mind is still confined to its physical conceptualities. However, man can assume that it is an existence where deserving souls flourish.

As a result, Jews view death with sadness, not with despair. They feel a great loss at losing loved ones, and they worry that their sins may lead to future punishment. But they face solace in the fact that death does not mean that a person becomes null and void. They are relieved that those who have suffered in illness now go on to a more peaceful state of being.

This is why the Jewish burial service is simple and dignified, rather than elaborate and gaudy. The departed's memory is sanctified through the eulogy and the recitation of the *Kaddish* by a close relative. The immediate family of the deceased sits *shiva* for seven days, during which friends visit them to comfort them and ease their grief. Every year, on the *yahrzeit* (the anniversary of the person's death), his family lights a candle in his memory, and *Kaddish* is said. Above all, the friends and family of the departed can pay their respects by learning Torah and performing good deeds in his memory. This is the most lasting of all tributes.

SUMMARY OF PART FOUR

In this section, we examined the rationale behind such Jewish laws as Shabbos, Yom Tov, Kashrus, Tefillah, Mezuzah, Tefillin, and *Tztizis. We also explored the status of women in Jewish law. We have seen how Jewish law helps man control his impulses and guides him toward a more sanctified life: how Shabbos makes him holy, how Kashrus purifies his body, and how Tefillah brings him closer to G-d. At the same time, Jewish laws, like the observance of Shabbos, Yom Tov, and Kashrus, help bring Jews together, and strengthen their national existence. Women are as important to the success of Judaism as men, and the fact that they are obligated to perform fewer Mitzvos than men only testifies to their importance to the household. Finally, Judaism has an optimistic view of death, believing that a spiritual World to Come awaits the righteous when they die.*

Next we will explore the relationships between Jews and non-Jews and the differences between Judaism and other religions.

PART FIVE

RELATIONS WITH THE GENTILE WORLD

PART FIVE: RELATIONS WITH THE GENTILE WORLD

Question Thirty-Two: Why are Jews discouraged from assimilating into gentile society? Doesn't Judaism believe in the brotherhood of man?

Answer: Judaism certainly believes that no group or race of men is inherently less intelligent or capable than others. All members of mankind are considered children of G-d, and all therefore have the opportunity to live decent, happy lives. Even non-Jews are expected to follow basic G-d-given precepts—the seven *Mitzvos Bnai Noach*—to enhance their existence. Judaism accords great respect to righteous gentiles, and refers to them as *"Chassidei Umos Ha'Olom"*.

At the same time, the Torah refers to the Jews as the Chosen People, the *Mamleches Kohanim* (nation of holy priests). They have a special innate potential for holiness, granted them by G-d. Consequently, they must make sure not to dilute this holiness. They must live up to the rigorous standards of the Torah. They must keep certain laws and avoid certain acts that gentiles need not worry about.

In practice, this means that the true Jewish lifestyle is in some ways very different from that of the gentile. True, both Jews and gentiles obtain educations, earn livings, and raise families. Jews can function in modern-day societies just as successfully as can anyone else. However, the Jew is given more specific instructions on how to obey G-d's will in achieving his life's goals. He is told to retain his innate spirituality through the laws of *Shabbos, Yom Tov, Kashrus, Tefillah,* and other commandments. If he does not—if he acts like a gentile, who is free of these commandments—he is forsaking his spiritual heritage. As a result, a Jew cannot live exactly as a gentile does, while still claiming to be a true Jew.

This does not, of course, mean that Jews and gentiles should have absolutely nothing to do with each other—though throughout history gentiles have often made sure that this was the case. Certainly, Jews and gentiles should—and often have—pooled efforts in the search for universal peace, human rights, and secure neighborhoods. Men must emphasize their similarities when it helps them live together in tranquility.

Whereas having neighborly relations is one thing though, intimate associations leading to assimilation is another. Those who try to assimilate often claim that they are only combining the best of Jewish and gentile cultures. However, the result is often a different one: a complete abandonment of the Jewish religion and loss of Jewish identity. In time, the assimilationists and their children come to forsake their Jewish names, their Jewish customs, and their Jewish heritage—in the process becoming more *'goyish'* than the gentiles they are emulating. They no longer bother to pay allegiance to the Torah, and laws of *Shabbos, Yom Tov,* and *Kashrus* fall by the wayside. They deny their children any form of Jewish education—because it is not "patriotic"—and they allow them to grow up ignorant of, and antagonistic to, Judaism. They give up a 4,000 year old pedigree—a chance to retain their G-dly spirituality—for the temporary glitter of the gentile world: the nightclubs, the country clubs, the discos, the "live-for-the-moment" experience.

There are always those who confidently claim that the above description does not apply to them; that they can retain their Jewishness—keep their Jewish names and education and membersip in synagogues—while still partaking fully of the *'goyish'* world. What they do not realize is that they are still diluting their special spirituality, that they are denying the unique Jewish character. How can the Jews be a *Mamleches Kohanim* if they must adopt the ways of the gentiles to feel fulfilled?

There are additional points to bear in mind, too. If one denies that he is a Jew, then what is he? It is common for people in today's depersonalized world to search for "roots"—for historical evidence that they belong to an ongoing group. They want to have pride in their past, and signs that their lineage is important. They want proof that they, indeed, command respect for their very existence. But what identity, what respect, can a lapsed Jew claim? What are his roots? What family can he turn to when the chips are down?

He should realize that whether he admits it or not, his Jewish background will not remain hidden. In times of crisis, gentiles always seem to know who has Jewish blood in him. As we mentioned before, estranged Jews have also been persecuted by anti-Semites. The Nazis did not differentiate between those Jews who were assimilated and those who weren't. Those who assimilate to feel safer are just deluding themselves. At least traditional Jews have the comfort of kinship to G-d and fellow Jews during the bad times. What do assimilated Jews have when their gentile friends turn on them?

What does the assimilated Jew accomplish? True, he might enjoy the luxuries of gentile society—for a while. But where has his Jewish spirituality gone to? What has happened to his holy heritage, his purpose for being? Can he ever be sure that he will not be treated by gentiles as an outsider? Will the sense of guilt, of split loyalties and inferiority complexes ever leave him? What will he do when he finally has to answer to G-d? Had he retained his faith, he could have at least felt an "insider" within Judaism, a member of a *Mamleches Kohanim*. He could have been guaranteed G-d's favor; he could have lived a holy life. And he could have done this easily in today's pluralistic society, where it is realized that differences help give one a sense of identity. He could have been proud to proclaim what he really is, but he chose not to. So, in the end, the assimilated Jew will stand alone, a pitiable figure—rich, perhaps; modern, maybe; but a man without a nation, a man without spirituality, a man without G-d.

Question Thirty-Three: Why does Judaism oppose intermarriage between Jews and gentiles?

Answer: In Judaism, marriage has a multifold purpose.

It is not just an emotional attachment, or a social convenience, though it certainly should satisfy emotional and social needs. It is also supposed to mark the establishment of a *Bayis Ne'eman B'Yisroel*"—a household worthy of G-d's blessing. It should be a union elevating each partner to greater spirituality, as well as allowing them to find happiness in harmony. The household is called a 'small *Beis Hamikdosh*', because of the holiness it gains, and because man and wife together can better serve G-d and Judaism. They can better perform such home-based *Mitzvos* as *Shabbos* and *Kashrus*. And they can establish a Jewish family—the backbone of the Jewish nation—and raise their children within the traditions of Judaism. However, all this can be accomplished only if both members of the partnership are Jewish. How can a household be called a miniature *Beis Hamikdosh* if one of its members is not a member of the *Am Hakodesh?* How can this be a union that enhances Judaism if even one partner is not Jewish? How can the tradition be handed down to children if there is no tradition to hand down?

The rising tide of intermarriage today holds disastrous consequences for the Jewish people. Every intermarriage presents the possibility that the Jewish partner will follow his gentile mate's ways, thus abandoning Judaism completely. He will no longer observe the Torah in the slightest; it will become a hindrance to his partner, and therefore, to himself. How can he keep *Shabbos* or *Kashrus* if his spouse doesn't cooperate? To preserve harmony at home, he may find it convenient to convert to another religion, or to ignore religion completely.

Furthermore, his children will most probably emerge as either non-Jews, or non-committed Jews. If the wife is the gentile partner, the children are legally *goyim*. If the husband is gentile, the children stand a good chance of copying his lifestyle. Either way, the Jewish partner will likely find his Jewish heritage ending with him. By intermarrying, he has broken the chain that bound him to countless generations of ancestors faithful to Judaism.

By choosing a gentile partner, the Jew is, in effect, rebelling against G-d. He denies the fact that the Jew is a G-dly being who, when united in marriage with a gentile, can no longer maintain his G-dly character. It is no wonder that the Rambam refers to intermarriage as a desertion of Judaism—among the worst of all sins.

In addition, intermarriages can pose personal problems for the partners involved. If a marriage works, it is often because the marriage partners have a great deal in common. They can share things with each other, and this can maintain a marriage beyond the time of physical infatuation. Partners of an intermarriage, though, may not always have that much to share. After all, members of different religions generally come from different backgrounds and environments. They have known different influences and have been directed towards different goals. Therefore, if a Jew and a gentile marry, they will probably have less in common than two Jews or two gentiles. Consequently, they may find themselves eventually incompatible. Furthermore, relations between the marriage partners and their respective in-laws are likely to be strained—a situation that will not help the marriage. True, it is possible that love may eventually conquer all the above obstacles, but why enter into a marriage with one or two strikes against it?

Furthermore, an intermarriage can create many emotional problems for the children it produces. Of course, if the intermarriage proves unsuccessful because of incompatibility, the offspring suffers the loss of a parent—a great psychological blow. Even if the marriage endures, the child may still face the question of his identity. As the product of Jewish and non-Jewish parents, he will come to wonder: What exactly am I? What will I claim as my background? What religion should I believe in? Should I celebrate Chanukah or Xmas? Should I follow Mom or Dad—and how can I please both? What should I raise my own children as? The emotional strain on such a child—often caught in a religious tug-of-war between parents—is usually great. Is it fair to subject him to such conditions?

Intermarriage is clearly a problem for the Jewish people. It can lead to unhappy marriages and produce confused youngsters. It leads to a shrinking of the Jewish population as a whole. Above all, it is a denial of the uniquely holy aspect of the Jewish people, and a desertion from G-d's religion. It is a cancer gnawing steadily away at Judaism's future.

Question Thirty-Four: How is Judaism different from the other major world religions?

Answer: Most scholars have included Judaism as one of five major world religions, the others being Hinduism, Buddhism, Islam and Christianity.

All religions claim to promote spirituality and inner peace, though whether this is always true is debatable. Most have sacred scriptures, and all involve prayer and belief. How, then, is Judaism unique?

Obviously, Judaism is the only religion which has been practiced by the Jewish nation throughout its existence allowing it to survive countless threats. Other religions have adopted tenets and rituals from Judaism, but Judaism was the original monotheistic religion. Judaism also differs from other religions in various basic ways, including the following:

a) **Hinduism**—Hinduism (or Brahmanism) is an ancient Eastern-based religion centered historically in India. It differs from Judaism in that it is polytheistic, with a belief in as many as 30 million gods, each with separate powers: a god for good and a god for bad. Judaism, on the other hand, recognizes only One all-encompassing G-d. In addition, Hinduism venerates certain living things, such as the cow, as being godly, whereas Judaism worships only G-d. Hinduism sees the world as an illusion, and life as basically evil, while Judaism views life as essentially good, for it is the creation of a benevolent Deity. Hinduism says that the ultimate goal of life is to obtain release from a constant cycle of death and rebirth of the self. It believes that the inner self (the Atman) is reincarnated in different generations until it has become entirely cleansed of sin. The practical result of this belief is the Caste System—the view that certain individuals are inherently inferior to others because they have sinned in previous lifetimes. The Caste System for centuries prevented the inclusion of the so-called "untouchables" into society—not on the basis of their own misdeeds, but solely in the belief that their basic selves were impure. Judaism, by way of contrast, emphasizes the unity of the Jewish people. While it may have different status levels *(Kohein, Levi, Yisroel),* this was only in regard to serving G-d in different ways. Within society itself, Jews are to be judged not on the basis of their birth, but on the basis of their deeds. In this way, even those from poor, humble families can become the most revered of leaders.

b) **Buddhism**—Buddhism is the religion of many people in Southeast Asia, including many in China and (in an altered form, Shintoism) in Japan. There are different varieties of Buddhism, such as Zen, Hinyana, and Mahayana Buddhism. In its original form, developed by a dissatisfied Hindu named Gautama, it believed in the continuous rebirth of the self (Karma). It adopted Hinduism's position that a person's lowly status in life indicated that he had done wrong during a previous lifetime. The only way for one to free his soul from continuous reincarnation, said Gautama, was to follow a Middle Way in life, essentially by conquering all personal desires. Man was to live according to an eight-fold path, stressing meditation and mental control, leading to what he claimed was an ultimate spiritual level called Nirvana.

Whereas Judaism certainly advises spiritual self-development in accordance with a "middle way", it also preaches a concern for one's fellow man rather than a total immersion in self. It believes that man can indeed improve his lot on this earth, and that every Jew should help his fellow man progress socially and religiously. Self-interest to the abandonment of others is merely selfishness.

In addition, Judaism places much more stress on laws and practices—concrete methods in which one can serve G-d and help others. Buddhism, on the other hand, does not recognize any gods, and its rituals are based largely on superstitions. Judaism provides a more tangible structure for worship and observance than these other religions.

c) **Islam**—Like Buddhism, this religion was formulated basically by one mortal individual, in this case a man named Mohammed. Before his advent, the Arabs were animists and polytheists. Mohammed, strongly influenced by Jews and Christians in Medina, adopted their belief in Monotheism, as well as certain other Jewish practices, such as praying several times a day, avoiding pork, giving alms to the poor, and observing a fasting period, called Ramadan.

On the other hand, Mohammed considered himself the prophet of G-d, despite the fact that Islam's history is not marked by the miraculous Divine revelations which distinguish Jewish history. Mohammed limited the practices required of Moslems, and Islam lacks the comprehensive law codes that give structure to Judaism.

Perhaps the most obvious difference between Judaism and Islam is the fact that the latter attempted to convert the rest of the world through force. Even during Mohammed's lifetime, his followers were on the march to spread Islam to the rest of the world, by all means possible. The Moslems conquered a great section of the eastern world, and came close to overrunning all of Europe—gaining most of their victories through bloodshed. Those who refused to convert to Islam were not looked upon favorably. This included the Jews, who were expected to convert by Mohammed himself, and who aroused his enmity when they refused to do so. In resorting to force to make others convert, Islam has been aggressive where Judaism has not. Judaism certainly does not coerce outsiders to join its ranks; it actually discourages insincere conversions, and abhors the use of bloodshed for any such goals.

d) **Christianity**—There are a wide variety of denominations within Christianity, each stressing its own brand of belief. Yet all basically stem from the preachings of a Jew named Jesus, as interpreted by another Jew named Saul (later Paul). Christianity can therefore trace its roots to Judaism, and some Christians claim to have inherited the Jews' mantle as G-d's Chosen People. They have adopted the *Chamishei Chumshei Torah* as their own, labeling them the "Old Testament"—but asserting that their "New Testament" is the natural follow-up. The Jews, on the other hand, feel that they remain what they always were—the Chosen People of the Bible—and that nothing has intervened since the giving of the Torah to have changed this.

At the center of this difference is the question of the status of the Jew, Jesus. Christianity claims that this individual was, in fact, not only the Jewish Messiah, but also the actual son of G-d (and, consequently, an aspect of G-d Himself). They claimed that he died to atone for mankind's sins, and that he will reappear on earth in a Second Coming. As this man's followers, Christians see themselves as the new promoters of G-d's will in the world, and some see it as their life's mission to convert as many members of mankind as possible to Christianity. Jews, while respecting the doctrines of love and peace, which Christianity claims as its basic tenets, rejects its basic notion that Jesus was anything more than a mere man who was killed. (We will examine the reasons for this view in the next question.) Consequently, Jews feel that belief in Jesus is misplaced, and that one should pray instead to G-d Himself. Jews see no need for any intermediary to G-d, nor do they feel that it is only through Jesus that man can atone. Rather, one can obtain atonement for his own misdeeds through prayer (see *Malochim* I 8:33-4), charity *(Tehilim* 21:3), and repentance *(Yermiyahu* 36:3)—by direct communication with G-d.

In practical terms, a major difference between the two religions is that Judaism accepts the Torah in its entirety, while Christianity does not. Despite the fact that Jesus was a Jew and advised adherence to the Torah's laws ("Think not that I have come to abolish the Law and the Prophets; I have come not to abolish them but to fulfill them. . . Whoever then breaks one of the least of these commandments and teaches men so shall be called least in the Kingdom of Heaven"—Matthew 5:17-19), Christians today do not practice such Torah laws as *Kashrus, Tefillin, Mezuzah,* and *Shabbos.* It was the belief of Paul, who developed the Christian religion, that the laws of the Torah were too difficult for the average Christian to observe. Instead, Christianity preaches that Faith and Love alone are sufficient to make one a good person.

Judaism certainly agrees that Love and Faith are essential if one is to be morally upright. The Torah was in fact the source for the precept of "Love Thy Neighbor" (*Vayikroh* 18:19). However, Judaism feels that general advice that one be kind and loving is in itself too vague and unfocused. One can easily claim to be a believer and still give in to animalistic urges. One can say "I love" and then commit rape and adultery. Christians have hardly remained true to their credo. Throughout history countless Jews have been killed because of the accusation that they were the "murderers of Jesus"; countless others died in the Inquisition's sadistic attempt to convert them to Christianity.

The Torah therefore lays down a more structured framework for love and kindness. "If there be among you a needy man. . . you shall surely open your hand to him," says the Torah in *Devorim* 15:7. "You shall not see your brother's donkey or ox fallen down by the way, and hide yourself from them; you shall surely help him to lift them up again (*Devorim* 22:4)." There are specific laws of charity, inviting guests, and visiting the sick. By specifying ways in which man can practice kindness, the Torah ensures these acts even when the person would not be inclined to do them on his own. This is why the Torah is a book not of harsh and restrictive law, but of loving legislation aimed at making man good. Furthermore, Judaism feels that these and other Torah laws are eternal, and cannot be abandoned under any conditions. They ensure that man show his faith in G-d through concrete, positive acts.

In sum, then, one can say that Judaism differs from other religions not only in that it is the tradition that has led to Jewish survival throughout history, but also in that it has always promoted faith in One G-d, has adhered to the laws of the Torah instead of in vague beliefs, has encouraged not only self-improvement but also the active aiding of others, and has not embarked on a war-like crusade to convert others to its ways. It is the sole life-plan that emanates directly from G-d. As Rav Samson Raphael Hirsch noted, in the case of other religions, man reached out for a god—but in Judaism, G-d reached out to man.

Question Thirty-Five: Why do Jews not accept Jesus as a god or a messiah?

Answer: Almost since the inception of Christianity, some Christians have made it their life's work to convert others, including Jews. At times, these missionaries have used torture and other coercions to gain their goal, such as during the Spanish Inquisition. More recently, Christian missionaries have employed different techniques—using friendly arguments and slick propaganda—for the same purpose. Missionaries have aggressively confronted Jews with misleading arguments and incorrect Biblical quotes. Lately, they have even resorted to using Jewish names and Hebrew songs to mislead Jews into thinking that they, too, are Jewish. Thus, we have the rise of the "Jewish Christians" who claim that the only "fulfilled" Jew is the one who believes in Jesus (called by them, "Yeshua").

Judaism respects the right of Christians to worship as they please. It, however, condemns those who try to impose Christianity on Jews through deceit or any other way. The missionaries show a dangerous degree of intolerance towards Judaism, implying that it is a false religion. Jews should therefore be ready to defend their religious beliefs, and to counteract missionary propaganda. Jews must know that missionary arguments can readily be answered, for they are misleading and based on false premises. Jews cannot sit idly by watching missionaries misleading their fellow religionists. There are too few Jews in the world today for us to afford defections to Christianity.

Missionaries say that Jesus is both the son of G-d and the long-awaited Messiah. Jews reject both claims, for the following reasons:

a) **No Man Can Be a G-d.** The Torah makes it clear that there is only one omnipotent, indivisible G-d: "The L-rd He is G-d; there is none else besides him" (*Devorim* 4:35)." G-d is unique unto

Himself, and does not consist of a trinity: "The L-rd He is G-d in heaven above and upon the earth below; there is none else" (*Devorim* 4:39). Jesus himself accepted G-d's uniqueness: "And he (Jesus) said unto him, 'Why callest thou me good? There is none good but one, that is, G-d." (Matthew 19:17). How, then, could a mortal man—one who was born and who died on a cross—be a segment of an immortal, indivisible G-d? There is no concept of infinity possible if G-d is a man or a Trinity. The Torah states clearly: "G-d is not a man" (*Bamidbar* 23:19).

b) **Jesus did not accomplish the tasks of the Messiah.** If Jesus had indeed been the Messiah, he would have fulfilled the Messianic prophecies mentioned in *Tanach*. For instance, the *Moshiach* (Messiah) will bring about universal peace and tranquility: "And they shall beat their swords into plowshares, and their spears into pruning hooks; nation shall not lift up sword against nation; neither shall they learn war any more" (*Yeshaya* 2:4). The *Moshiach* will bring about universal respect for G-d, and lead all people to follow His ways: "The knowledge of G-d will fill the earth. The world will be filled with the knowledge of G-d as the water covers the sea" (*Yeshaya* 11:9). He will cause an ingathering of the Jewish exiles: "Then the residue of his brethren shall return with the children of Israel" (*Micha* 5:2) and will bring about the rebuilding of the *Beis Hamikdosh*:. "In that day will I raise up the Tabernacles of David that is fallen" (*Amos* 9:11). He will also bring physical cure to all who are sick: "Then the eye of the blind will be opened, and the ears of the deaf will be unstopped. Then the lame man will leap as a hart, and the tongue of the dumb will sing" *(Yeshaya* 35:5-6). Furthermore, he will accomplish these tasks within his own lifetime: "He shall not fail or be crushed until he has set the right in the earth" (*Yeshaya* 42:4).

The clear-cut fact is that Jesus did *not* fulfill any of these tasks. The *Beis Hamikdosh* has not been rebuilt, and the Jews are still in exile. (Incidentally, it is hard to see how Jesus could rebuild the *Beis Hamikdosh* or return the Jews to Israel when the *Beis Hamikdosh* was still in existence and the Jews were still in Israel during his lifetime.) Suffering and pain still abound, and the world is certainly less religiously-inclined today than it was during Jesus's day. Immorality, corruption, and crime are definitely in evidence to this very day, and the past 2,000 years have seen one war after another.

If the Messiah has already come, why is the world in such a sad state?

Christian theology has come up with the explanation that Jesus will reappear during a Second Coming, when he will finally fulfill the Messianic prophecies. But there is no reference to such a delayed second coming of the same Messiah anywhere in the Torah. Jesus himself promised his followers that he would succeed in his own era: "Verily I say to you that there be some of them who stand here, which shall not taste of death until they have seen the kingdom of G-d come with power" (Mark 9:1); "Verily I say to you that this generation shall not pass, till all these things be done" (Mark 13:30). But the things were *not* done, and Jesus was instead killed.

c) **Jesus did not keep Jewish law.** The *Moshiach* is expected to keep all the laws of the Torah, and to inspire others to do likewise. (See *Devorim* 13). However, at times Jesus considered himself to be above the law: "For the Son of Man is master even of the Sabbath" (Matthew 12:8). He broke the laws of the Sabbath—part of the Ten Commandments—and reviled the Rabbis, who are accorded great respect by the Torah. Jesus did not even always espouse peace: "Think not that I am come to send peace on earth; I came not to send peace, but a sword" (Matthew 10:34). Can one who *denies* G-d's sacred law be His Messiah?

d) **Lack of Jewish support.** Jesus lived at the time of Roman suppression of the Jews. The Jewish people eagerly looked forward to the arrival of the *Moshiach.* They were certainly well-versed in the requirements to be filled by the true *Moshiach,* and would definitely have accepted the *Moshiach* if it was clear that he had appeared. Yet the Jews of that time—and especially the learned Sages—rejected Jesus's claims to be the Messiah. They knew and saw Jesus in the flesh, and found him wanting; on the other hand, Paul of Tarsus, who established the Christian religion, never knew Jesus personally. If Jesus were indeed the Messiah, why did his fellow Jews, who had every reason to want a Messiah, almost unanimously reject him?

Missionaries often say that they have Biblical proof of Jesus's divinity or Messianic role. However, these arguments often rely on misquotes and faulty reasoning.

One such "proof" comes from *Yeshaya* 7:14, which they translate as follows: "Behold the virgin is with child, and she will bear a son, and his name will be called Immanu-el." The unsuspecting individual might think that this is a prophecy of the New Testament's account of Jesus's birth. However, one who studies the verse in its original Hebrew will note that the term used is "*almah*", which means "young woman", not "virgin". (The Hebrew word for virgin is "*besulah*", as mentioned in Vayikroh 21:3). In any case, the verse refers to the birth of King Chezkiah, and has nothing at all to do with the *Moshiach*.

Another supposed "proof" is the verse in *Micha* 5:1: "But you, Bethlehem Ephrasah, which are little to be among the thousands of Judah, out of you shall come forth onto Me that is to be ruler in Israel, whose going forth are from old, from ancient days." Missionaries claim that this refers to Jesus, who they say was born in Bethlehem. But the verse really refers to the fact that the *Moshiach* will come from the lineage of King David, who was born in Bethlehem. And Christians cannot claim that Jesus came from King David, for the lineage follows the father, and they say that Jesus had *no* earthly father.

Finally, there is the so-called "proof" from *Yeshaya* 53, which refers to a "Suffering Servant". Missionaries will say that this means Jesus, who suffered on the cross. But the term "servant", when used elsewhere in *Yeshaya,* refers to the Jewish nation, whose members are G-d's dedicated servants. They have certainly suffered throughout the years—yet they have survived for a long time, unlike Jesus, who died childless at the age of 33, and the verse refers to the servant's prolonged days and "seed" (children).

There are other such arguments, with accurate and concise Jewish responses to each. All Jews must be aware that missionary claims should not be taken at face value, and that the Jewish rejection of the Messiahship of Jesus has a sound Biblical basis.

SUMMARY OF PART FIVE

In this section, we viewed Judaism in relationship to the gentile society. We saw how Judaism is unique in its being the religion of G-d's Chosen People, who are expected to obey special laws and maintain special standards. We noted that Judaism shares the concern of the other major religions for love, peace, and spirituality, but we added that Judaism feels that man can best attain these goals through the legal structure described in the Torah. In contrast, most other religions provide for only vague suggestions as to how one can practice love and faith.

Because Judaism is unique, Jews should be proud to retain their Jewishness. We therefore said that Judaism frowns on assimilation into the gentile mainstream, and on intermarriage. Jews can certainly become highly respected members of the general society, and can take part in its operations. But Jews should not abandon their own roots and identity just to seek the friendship of the gentile world. History has shown that, in the long run, a Jew can count on only his fellow Jews during times of need.

Now we will turn to a final question: How can one be a better Jew? How can one improve himself to live up to the high standards requested by G-d? The next section offers some specific suggestions.

PART SIX

SELF-IMPROVEMENT

PART SIX: SELF-IMPROVEMENT

Question Thirty-Six: How can one go about becoming a better Jew?

Answer: Asking this question is itself a step in the right direction.

Allowing ones self to stagnate is a common problem. Even the most pious of Jews can make the mistake of letting the status quo remain the final word. The fact is that there are very, very few among us who cannot become better Jews. There is always room for improvement. One who does not progress as a person is in reality regressing. As *Pirkei Avos* says, " He who does not increase (his knowledge of Judaism) decreases from it" (*Avos* 1:13).

Therefore, if one wants to improve himself as a Jew, and to better himself as a person, he is already moving toward his goal. He should realize that this will require a stiff effort, and that he will face problems—that "it is not easy to be a Jew". Nevertheless, if he wants to learn more about his religion, and to adopt a Jewish identity and lifestyle, he already deserves G-d's favor.

If willingness to improve is a first step, what comes next? A positive attitude is a necessary prerequisite. But what will make the quest successful is positive action—becoming actively involved in the world of Judaism.

The following are some suggestions on making the journey to self-improvement a smooth one:

1. **Studying Judaism.** Before one can become a good Jew, he should know what this means. The best way to learn this is to study the encyclopedic Life Guide for Jews—the Torah. As we have already mentioned, the Torah contains not only the basic laws of Judaism, but also the inspiring story of the Jewish people, their purpose in life, and their ultimate goals. One's course in Judaism should also include other sources of insight into Judaism. These include the *Talmud,* with its wellsprings of Torah laws, knowledge, and discussions of morality (*Pirkei Avos* is a particularly helpful guide to the basis of Jewish moral philosophy); the various law codes (such as the *Shulchan Oruch* and the *Mishna Berurah*); the philosophical dissertations of the Sages (see the bibliography for

several such works available in English); books of Jewish history, told from a traditional viewpoint (to gain a perspective of the Jewish role in history); and books of *Mussar*, and self-improvement (such as those by the Chofetz Chaim, which point out ways in which all Jews can correct personal defects in their character).

No one can claim that he has totally mastered all Torah literature, and no one can say that he cannot learn any further ways to better himself from it.

2. **Learning from beneficial influences.** Studying in isolation can often be frustrating. What if one becomes bored, or what if one has questions? Who can stimulate him further, and who can explain what he cannot understand?

That is why one should seek out mentors, or even friends, with whom to learn about Judaism. This can mean joining a *shiur* or a small study group, or even forming a simple partnership with one other person for the purpose of learning Torah together. The interaction between two individuals trying to understand the Torah's admonitions for proper living can be extremely stimulating, and very fruitful.

However, one does not have to learn only from the written page. One can learn as much from another Jew's demeanor as he can from his words. It is said that the students of one Chassidic leader flocked to him, not just to hear him discuss the Torah, but also to see him tie his shoelaces. They knew that his everyday manner of living contained more lessons for them than they could learn in any number of lectures. We are influenced by what we see, and we copy whom we admire.

That is why one must be careful when choosing his close companions. If one notices that those around him are harmful influences, he should seek different company. He should associate with those who will set a good Torah-based example for him. He should seek out guidance from the Gedolim (sages of the day). He can then learn from their example—and, in due time, can set the same example for others.

3. **Joining Jewish groups.** One way of coming into the right company is by actively seeking it out. One should take the positive step of joining worthwhile Jewish groups, and becoming actively

involved in them. This does not mean that he should merely add his name to the membership lists, and feel fulfilled with that. Absentee membership means nothing.

What one has to do is to locate those groups that are really helping the Jewish people, and to offer them whatever services he can. He should become an active participant in a traditional shul, and he should send his children to a yeshiva for a sound Jewish education. He should feel obliged to participate in their *Tzedokoh* drives, and he should take part in their efforts to help in the local community. This way, he will consider himself a full-fledged member of the Jewish people, working directly for the betterment of his fellow Jews, never having to worry about loneliness or lack of direction in life.

4. **Doing Mitzvos.** We have seen that the Jewish religion is a very practical one. It has a set of positive deeds—the *Mitzvos*—which give man a chance to actively help others, and thereby, himself; and to openly display his allegiance to G-d. They are meant to be studied, but—more importantly—they are meant to be performed.

Therefore, one should perform the *Mitzvos* as sincerely as he can. He should understand the concepts behind *Mitzvos* like *Tefillin, Tzitizis, Kashrus, Mezuzah*—and he should participate in them. He should especially partake in *Mitzvos* relating to others: helping the poor, visiting the sick, befriending the lonely. Giving charity is laudable—but as commendable as signing a check is, it is the direct involvement with the poor and the needy that provides the greatest fulfillment. In showing concern for others—new immigrants, new adherents to traditional Judaism—one should not sit back and wait for opportunities, but he should take the initiative. Inviting other Jews to one's home for *Shabbos,* or initiating newcomers to the ways of Judaism, are primary examples of positive steps to be taken.

The more one becomes involved in doing *Mitzvos,* the more one feels a partner in the progress of the Jewish nation.

5. **Viewing life from a Jewish viewpoint.** One who thinks deeply about life—its meaning and its purpose—will come to the realization that G-d is just, and that His laws are valid. True, he may

face opposition from others, who might ridicule him for his beliefs and his lifestyle, but that shouldn't deter him. One who knows that he is right can persevere against scorn. He can lead his life from a uniquely Jewish perspective, constantly asking himself, "How would G-d want me to behave in this case?" He should wonder if developments are helpful to the Jewish nation, and if he is doing all to help his fellow Jews. He should remember that this world is not a be-all and end-all in itself, but a pathway to a higher existence. In short, he should always remember that he is, first and foremost, a Jewish human being—and act accordingly.

It is hoped that this series of questions and answers about Judaism has made the reader more aware of Jewish living—its rationale, and its advantages. Perhaps he has gained a more solidly-based faith in G-d, and a deeper appreciation of the Torah and its laws. Above all, it is hoped that it has inspired him to become a better Jew, in his beliefs and his actions.

If Jews around the world take a deeper look at the benefits and foundations of their religion, maybe they will all accept it with greater fidelity.

This may in turn prompt G-d to send us the Moshiach and to restore the Beis Hamikdosh within the very near future.

Let us so hope, and pray.

BIBLIOGRAPHY

This book should be supplemented by other works to afford the reader a well-rounded view of Judaism.

We strongly suggest that the reader carefully study the basic Jewish holy texts—the *Tanach* and the *Talmud*—in their original Hebrew, for a full appreciation of Jewish thought and law.

We also heartily recommend the *Art Scroll* series of works from the *Tanach* and *Mishnayos*, with full translation and commentaries by highly-regarded Torah scholars.

The following is a not exhaustive list of English-language texts which the reader should find very useful in supplementing the basic Torah works.

HASHKOFOH (JEWISH PHILOSOPHY)

Rabbi Eliyahu Dessler, *Strive For Truth,* Feldheim, Publishers, 1978
Rabbi Zechariah Fendel, *Anvil Of Sinai,* Hashkafah Publications, 1977
Rabbi Zechariah Fendel,*Challenge Of Sinai,* Hashkafah Publication, 1978
Paul Forchheimer, *Living Judaism,* Feldheim Publishers, 1977
Rabbi Samson Raphael Hirsch, *The Nineteen Letters,* Feldheim Pub., 1969
Rabbi Yehuda Halevi, *The Kuzari* (A. Davis, ed.)
Rabbi Naftoli Hoffner, *Our Life's Aim,* Mosad Eliezer, Hoffner, 1978
Rabbi Aryeh Kaplan, *Handbook of Jewish Thought,* Maznaim Publishing Co, 1979
Rabbi Eliyahu Lopian, *Lev Eliyahu,* Pinsk, 1975
Rabbi Moshe Maimonides (Rambam), *The Faith Of A Jew,* Jewish Pocket Books (also see other volumes in the series)
Rabbi Avigdor Miller, *Rejoice O Youth,* 1962
Rabbi Avigdor Miller, *Sing Ye Righteous,* 1973
Mayer Schiller, *The Road Back,* Feldheim Publishers, 1979
Avi Shafran, *Jewthink,* Herman Press, 1977

CHUMASH

Rabbi Samson Raphael Hirsch, *Pentateuch,* (5 volumes), Judaica Press, 1963
Rabbi M. Miller, *Sabbath Shiurim* (2 volumes)
Rabbi Eli Munk, *The Call Of The Torah,* Feldheim Publishers, 1980
Rabbi Eli Munk, *The Seven Days Of The Beginning,* Feldheim Publishers, 1974

SIDDUR

Chofetz Chayim, *Chofetz Chayim On The Siddur,* Feldheim, 1974
Chofetz Chayim, *On Wings Of Prayer*
Rabbi Eli Munk, *World Of Prayer,* Feldheim Publishers

MITZVOS

Dayan I. Grunfeld, *The Dietary Laws,*Soncino Press, 1972
Dayan I. Grunfeld, *The Sabbath,* Feldheim Publishers, 1959
Rabbi Samson Raphael Hirsch, *Horeb (2 volumes),* Soncino Press, 1972
Rabbi Aryeh Kaplan, *Tefillin,* N.C.S.Y.
Rabbi Aryeh Kaplan, *Waters of Eden,* N.C.S.Y.
Rabbi A.E. Kitov, *The Jew and His Home,* Shengold Publishers, 1963
Rabbi Zelig Pliskin, *Love Your Neighbor,* Aish HaTorah Publications, 1977

JEWISH WOMEN

Rabbi B. Eisenberg, *Guide for the Jewish Woman and Girl*
Moshe Meiselman, *Jewish Women in Jewish Law,* Ktav, 1978

JEWISH HISTORY

Rabbi Philip Biberfeld, *Universal Jewish History,* Feldheim Pub., 1973
Rabbi Joseph Elias, *The Spirit of Jewish History,* Jewish Pocket Books
Rabbi Avigdor Miller, *Behold a People,* 1968
Rabbi Avigdor Miiler, *Torah Nation, 1971*
Harry Schimmel, *The Oral Law,* Feldheim, 1971

CHRISTIANITY

Rabbi Aryeh Kaplan, *The Real Messiah,* N.C.S.Y., 1973
J. Levy,ed., *The Disputation,* ScholarlyPublications, 1972

SCIENCE

Yaakov Kornreich, ed., *A Science and Torah Reader* N.C.S.Y., 1970
John Moore, and Harold Slusher, *Biology: A Search for Order in Complexity,* (Public School Edition), Zondervan Publ.,1974
*Judaism and Science,*Jewish Pocket Books